Between TWO Worlds

Between TWO Worlds

Lessons from the Other Side

Tyler Henry

GALLERY BOOKS

New York   London   Toronto   Sydney   New Delhi

Contents

Introduction

More than ever, people are coming forward and sharing their experiences with after-death communication. Through television and film, the question of whether life exists beyond death has captivated our popular culture—not because it's a new question, but because people are opening their minds to new answers. When I first got the call that my television show, *Hollywood Medium with Tyler Henry*, had been green-lighted, I promised to make it my purpose to explore whatever answers came my way and to share them honestly with the world. That's the mission I'm still on, and my own questions multiply by the day. With all the different opinions about mediumship and psychic phenomena in circulation, I aim to provide unique, easy-to-understand explanations, obtained through my firsthand experiences.

I'm a firm believer that people should be able to decide for themselves what resonates with them. I'll share what I've learned through communicating with the other side, and I encourage you to take from it what resonates with *you*. When it comes to the hereafter—things aren't black or white. Taking into account the gray areas in between, I'll explain some of the more consistent dynamics I've observed over the course of more than a thousand readings. There are many exceptions to the rules, but that's the beauty of the other side. It's far more complex and nuanced than anything we as humans can comprehend. There are some big questions to which I may never have the answers. However, every small answer helps contribute to our understanding of a much larger question: what happens when we die?

I speak to dead people. More interestingly, the dead speak back to me—primarily through sending mental impressions and sensations from the other side. All of what I do revolves around validation—that is, getting the confirmation from the sitter that the information I'm receiving is accurate and could only be known by the communicating spirit. Upon validation, my client gets the knowledge that their loved one's soul continues on, is at peace, and is able to communicate anything that had been left unsaid or that was realized during the transitioning process.

If there's anything I've learned through my work, it's that in life, diversity is a gift. I know many different kinds of people will be drawn to this book, from all different backgrounds, belief systems, and degrees of familiarity with the subject matter. In the following pages, I'll share with you my spiritual beliefs. However, I think it's more important for you to understand the process of exactly what happens when a spirit comes through. For that reason, I'll focus on the details of the experiences, so you can draw your own conclusions about how it all fits into the big picture of *your* beliefs. Individual differences aside, I think we can agree that we all benefit from the healing of others and the idea that love is eternal. The goal of my work, and the work of many other authentic mediums, is to reinforce these universal truths.

I understand that my ability is a gift and not something for which I can take any credit. I'm just a conduit for information to come through and reach those who are open to hearing it—something we all have a natural ability to do, to varying degrees. Practice breeds consistency, and the more we develop and trust in our gut feelings, the more significantly and accurately our intuition can help us. Even after doing countless readings, I still have to remind myself daily to "get out of my own way" and allow myself to be a clear vessel through which messages can flow.

When I first started learning about my abilities, I spent endless hours at bookstores and libraries, reading multiple books a day, and searching the Internet for resources and information about what made me so different. Being the only one experiencing an entirely other world was alienating in the truest sense.

I felt like I had one foot in this world and one in the next. I didn't understand, nor did I feel understood by, either side. As a kid, learning the ropes to our earthly dimension was challenging enough, let alone throwing another one into the mix. I was somewhere in between, a messenger in the middle of two realms: a medium.

Throughout my life, I've come to understand the world in two ways. In one sense, I'm like any other twenty-year-old adjusting to adulthood, learning to live on my own (and use a dishwasher for the first time, admittedly). Yet in a very different sense, the part of me that most people see is Tyler Henry the medium—the Macaulay Culkin look-alike who gets in touch with celebrities' dead loved ones on television. Though most people can't relate to what it's like to get visual, sensorial, and mental impressions from people who've passed away, everyone is capable of understanding the impact those messages have on the loved ones who need it most. Whether it's a reference to pink fuzzy dice from your aunt Edna, or an inside joke shared with a beloved grandmother, these are the messages I strive to deliver—no matter how random they may seem to me, personally.

When my clients come for a reading, I view my connecting process as a bit of a puzzle to solve. I receive impressions from one or more spirits, and together, the querent and I establish how the message is relevant and where it connects. Readings are 50 percent receiving the information and 50 percent untangling it. Throughout the past few years of doing sessions, I've seen countless forms of healing result from validating messages. Whether it's closure from a loved one, much-needed proof of a hunch, or a release of guilt, I've been able to see what makes the most life-changing differences in each after-death communication. With each contact I make, I aim to bring a loved one through so clearly that it's undoubtable to my client that I'm connecting. This validation comes from describing personality traits, quirks, family traditions, inside references, and sometimes even physical mannerisms. It's the small, but specific, details that communicate the essence of who someone is in life, and the same can be true for those on the other side.

Every day brings new experiences and new stories shared by souls that are able to understand what truly mattered in their lives. Their messages teach us what we should value in our own. Above all, I've learned that transitioning to the other side gives perspective. Ironically enough, it's the dead who have the most to teach us about life.

In this book, I hope to provide the reader with a narrative unlike any other—one that's honest, down-to-earth, and uses terms everyone can understand. Besides answering some frequently asked questions, I want to delve into all areas of my human experience—as well as those of the individuals, living and dead, whose paths I've crossed.

1

The Beginning

I cried out, "Mom, we have to say goodbye to Grandma!" Surprised by my own words, I paused before continuing, "We have to go *now*. She's going to die *tonight*."

I stumbled into the kitchen and stood beside my mother. I felt an overwhelming urgency. I had just woken up with a total certainty that my beloved grandmother was going to pass away. It felt like a memory, only it hadn't happened yet. Wordlessly, my mother grabbed her phone and purse and headed toward the door. As I followed her, time seemed to slow. I felt a sense of loss flooding and ebbing through me, in debilitating waves. I knew I absolutely needed to say goodbye to my grandmother; I also knew that we didn't have much time.

As we hurried to the car, my mother's phone rang. A feeling of familiarity nagged at me. What started as an unexplainable certainty was now becoming a reality before my eyes: my mom answered the call, and she was informed that my grandmother had taken her final breath only moments before.

At ten years old, I'd just had my first experience with what could only be described as a "knowingness." This feeling wasn't just a hunch. It was a conviction that did not waver, despite not understanding from where it had come. Since that day, a bizarre knowingness would change every aspect of life and death, as I came to understand them. Having never learned before what precognition or intuition is, I was deeply confused by what happened. Why had I awoken in a manner unlike anything I'd ever experienced—imparted with unknowable information and an urgent need to communicate it?

Ultimately, my grandmother's death affected my life more than anyone could have imagined at the time. As my family grieved, I was unable to forget the feeling I'd experienced that night. The people around me cried, but I couldn't bring myself to feel the same way they did. Somehow, having advance knowledge that she was going to transition—even though it was only by a few moments—entirely changed the way I processed the news of her death. Because I had experienced the future as the past, I understood on a deep level that the outcome couldn't have been prevented. More than needing any comforting, I found myself consoling my parents.

I was not surprised that my mom didn't tell my dad about my premonition. With almost no understanding of the experience myself, my parents were even less likely to comprehend it. What did surprise me was one memory that replayed through my mind. It was of my mom grabbing her things and rushing through the door, heeding my warning without hesitation. Did she have a "knowingness" herself, that what I had said was true?

The next evening, as I settled into bed, I lay down and closed my eyes. After the harrowing previous twenty-four hours, I tried to quiet my emotions. As I began dozing off, I noticed a sweet fragrance wafting into the room. It was distinctly familiar. In my half-conscious state, I realized that this scent was the same flowery perfume my grandmother wore when I was a little boy.

Lying there, I recalled the happy memories we'd shared and how prominent that smell had been. I squeezed my eyes shut. I was afraid that if I opened them, this precious connection to my grandmother would dissipate. I felt myself slipping into the edge of a dream.

Suddenly, I was jolted awake with a feeling of total alertness. *I was not alone in my room.* Just as my eyes adjusted to the darkness, a light appeared. Was it a car's headlights beaming in from the street? I rubbed my eyes. Standing at the foot of my bed appeared a figure. It looked like a considerably younger version of my newly deceased, elderly grandmother. To this day, I am amazed by how calm my ten-year-old self was about this event. My dead grandmother was standing at the foot of my bed, smiling, and enveloped in golden light. Though she looked forty years younger than I'd ever seen her, her essence was unmistakable.

I was enthralled by her radiance. Before her death, having battled cancer for months, she lost all of her hair and was unable to get out of bed. As I saw her now, she had beautiful, lightly curled blond hair, youthful rosy cheeks, and kind eyes. I was seeing her as she saw herself. Before I had time to process what was happening, my thoughts were interrupted by a voice that I'd known my entire life.

"There won't be much, but the necklace in the brown box is yours," she said. "It's just stuff. I will see you again."

I stared in astonishment. How casual she seemed, and her demeanor was as soft as it had been in life. Her voice was the kind, comforting sound that was so familiar to me. The light around her expanded, and she stepped forward. I felt her warm embrace around me and her wordless message: her love for me transcended death itself.

I had known my grandmother for only a decade of her life, yet her presence seemed to communicate a whole lifetime of memories. It was an experience I treasure to this day. Not only did I get closure, but I gained perspective. I saw her in a way I never had. Though our visit was brief, so many vivid flashes came through, just by being around her. Up until that point, I had never understood that messages could be delivered without words. These messages came in the form of pictures, which initially had little personal meaning: a gold necklace in a wood box, which transformed into a colorful ladybug and a burst of red roses. I had no control over or understanding of these images. They appeared in my mind as vividly as a fresh memory.

Seemingly as soon as it started, my visit with my grandmother was finished. I experienced the emptiness of my room— the previous warmth of reconnection that had flowed through it for a surreal moment came to an abrupt end. Those minutes had felt timeless, as though I had been transported into eternity itself. Now the light that had just given me so much joy contrasted sharply with darkness. In an odd way, this moment felt like her second death. Years later, I would come to learn that some who transition don't visit their loved ones immediately after passing. They don't want to make an unprepared loved one feel a second wave of loss when the visitation ends. Ultimately, I believe the departed know how far along we are in our grief process and our readiness to receive their signs. On the other hand, as part of a soul's process in finding resolution, they will sometimes communicate messages to their loved ones as a means of getting closure for *themselves*.

As I lay awake trying to process what I had just experienced, the question crossed my mind whether to tell my parents about the visitation. I knew that I had to be careful at such a sensitive time, with no idea how they'd respond. My dead grandmother had visited me in a waking dream, and I had no doubt it was a real interaction that took place. This was my first spiritual awakening—not to mention a literal awakening. I felt appreciative to have had such definite connection and closure with the first loved one I'd experienced losing. Yet her visit left me with far more questions than answers.

I'd had no prior discussions with my family about souls being able to communicate after death. I didn't know whether my parents would find my interaction to be comforting or disturbing, especially in light of having predicted my grandmother's passing. I knew that both my parents attended church and that my extended family was deeply religious, with rigid beliefs. I struggled to fit my experience into their framework. If after death there is only heaven and hell, how was my newly deceased grandmother in my room?

At the time, I concluded it was safest to keep my visions to myself. I began digging for answers on my own. I couldn't help but wonder, with all of the messages my grandmother could communicate, why the emphasis on a necklace? Especially one I didn't even know existed, and in a message that made little sense? We'd shared a decade's worth of memories, but she didn't mention a single one. Instead, she emphasized not getting caught up on material "stuff." This was confusing, because—being ten and not particularly sentimental—I didn't feel a need to have anything of my grandmother's to remember her by, much less get caught up about.

This would foreshadow a lifetime of readings in which messages would come through, for which I simply couldn't understand the context. Time and time again, I would be taught that context isn't essential to being a conduit. Trusting that what I was interpreting intuitively was factual—without analysis—was the first step required in putting the validity of the messages to the test.

Over the next few days, my family prepared for my grandmother's funeral. At the church, as people filled the pews, I felt no need to be there. Only a few days earlier, I had experienced the most profound closure for which a person could ask. Though I didn't fully understand what my experience meant, I never questioned how real it was. Throughout the service, I observed people whom I didn't know speaking about my grandmother in heartfelt eulogies. As I watched each person go to the stage, I understood how my best friend, advocate, and the human being I was closest to had changed the lives of everyone she touched. Their eyes communicated a loss that words couldn't do justice. That didn't stop them from trying, though. As for my grandmother's spirit? It was nowhere to be seen. I realized in that moment that funerals are really for the living.

We made our way to the cemetery, and my cousin sat beside me. Soon, a ladybug landed on her finger, and it perched there throughout the entire service. When she would try to shake it off, it would stubbornly fly back onto her hand, and then onto mine. It was almost comically persistent. We were paying more mind to this clingy bug than we were to the preacher at the podium. By the end of the service, my aunt had noticed how distracted we were. She suggested that the ladybug may have been a sign from my grandmother. As soon as she spoke the words, chills traveled down my spine. It's the same sensation I'll get today, when a message is validated as being correct. As we exited the service, dozens of red roses lay before my grandmother's casket. I felt the same chill as before. Two of the three visions I'd received had immediate relevance, within minutes of each other. What did the rest of her message mean? How did it all fit into what felt like the strangest puzzle ever?

A few days passed, and it was time to go to my grandmother's home. We planned to distribute her possessions among close family. Though she wasn't wealthy, she took care of what she did have, and she valued sharing it with her grandchildren. I headed up the same porch stairs where I had first learned to walk, and I remembered the summers we spent together. We would sit out on the porch playing board games or go for strolls during sunset. This was the family's first time being back at her home since she passed. We couldn't help but feel nostalgic, but it was short-lived. When we opened the front door, we found almost all of her belongings to be entirely missing. We later learned that a distant family member and his wife had stripped the property of everything they could find. My close family was absolutely gutted to realize that along with the things with monetary value, also taken were things that mattered far more to us: the inexpensive, sentimental objects that held value money couldn't buy. With a mix of sadness, grief, anger, and frustration, my family looked around for any sentimental items by which we could remember my grandmother. Photographs that we had grown up around suddenly became coveted objects. An aura of desperation permeated the house, as we walked through it for the last time. As we did a final sweep of the premises, my cousin announced from the other room that she had found a wood jewelry box under the bed. I ran into the room and opened the box. Inside was a single piece of jewelry—a gold pendant and chain.

As I held the necklace that my grandmother had indicated was meant to be mine, I was overcome with emotion. In a series of flashes, the images that she had communicated to me ran through my mind. I understood exactly what she had meant to tell me. The red roses were her way of acknowledging that she knew she was loved, because dozens of them were placed by those who knew and cared for her. The ladybug was a reminder that she was always with us. Most profoundly, my grandmother had acknowledged that she knew that certain family members would plunder her belongings for their own gain, rather than coming together as a family during a time of loss. In that way, she reassured us that the disappointing choices of the living didn't disturb her sense of peace on the other side.

It was in that moment that I understood that symbols, and their contexts, often convey messages far deeper and more profound than they appear. More than anything, it showed me that my urgent desperation to say goodbye to my grandmother the night she passed—a feeling to which so many can relate when facing loss—hadn't been necessary. Dying doesn't mean having to say goodbye.

In the years following my grandmother's death, life was very different. I went through my day conscious of the world around me, but I began experiencing new impressions and images. They varied in consistency—sometimes they came as I dreamed, sometimes while awake. Sometimes I'd see many in a day; other times, weeks could pass without any notable visions or insights. I sort of knew, or suspected, what was happening. However, it was only a bizarre, seemingly random ability. There was no instructional manual to tell me what it was or how to use it.

I was thankful I had closure with my grandmother, but I was also surprised that she hadn't delivered any messages intended for my mom or dad. They were still deeply grieving her loss. As I would later learn, some individuals go through a process after death, in which they "go quiet" from this realm. They undertake their process on the other side, which involves reviewing their lifetime to gain deeper understanding into the impact they'd made. The time this process takes is different for every individual, depending on how they adjust after passing. I've learned that it can be completely normal after dying to feel disconnected from your loved ones, for various reasons. In other cases, people do feel signs from their loved one shortly after passing. How an individual on the other side chooses to connect will vary. I'm constantly surprised by how much spirits reflect the essence of who they were in life.

Though few familiar faces ever came through to me, many strangers did. They tried to share messages with me, sometimes unsuccessfully. Most of these early visions came in a form we're all familiar with: dreams. My middle school years were filled with night terrors and frustrating dreams that were more exhausting than being awake, due to the fact that I was lucid throughout many of them. On the rare mornings when I wouldn't remember a dream from the previous night, I felt a brief sense of normalcy and relief. Being transported into various situations with crystal clear lucidity was intriguing at first, but it quickly grew to feel more like a nuisance than a useful ability. All I wanted was relief.

One morning, I woke after a woman had visited me with a specific message for my mother. I was in a deep sleep and lucid as usual, when a short-haired brunette woman appeared in front of me. She was not much older than my parents. Unlike the youthful way my grandmother presented herself in my first vision, this woman projected the age she was when she died. Unsure whether she would speak, I took in as many clues as I could about this woman's life or what led to her death. I couldn't help but notice a pair of dangling earrings that nearly reached to her shoulders. She was clothed in fabrics of various colors, and I was fascinated by how intricate and detailed she was in her appearance. I was particularly intrigued by the fact that those who would visit me nightly were dressed as though they had never died. Of all my questions, I was most curious and baffled by the fact that spirits appeared wearing specific clothing.

No, the spirit world doesn't produce polyester. As I would later find out, the way a medium sees a spirit has everything to do with how that spirit chooses to present. Generally, souls will come through in ways that are relatable to us. Just like in life, how someone chooses to appear can provide intimate details into their personality.

In the case of the woman who stood in front of me, I could tell by the bright colors her spirit adorned itself with that she was what you'd call "a character." In a raspy voice, she said, "Tell your mom there's a flower for her at my funeral. She'll know."

Before I had time to process the message or ask for additional details, I was jolted awake. My face was hot and sweaty. Groggily, I opened my eyes, and the sun was beaming in through my window. My mom barged into my room, as she often did. Not wanting to forget my message—and entirely without thinking—I blurted out what I had seen and heard only moments ago. What followed was one of the turning points in our relationship, as she got validation in one of the most personal ways possible.

As the hair on my mom's arms stood up, her face changed from looking preoccupied to being entirely attentive. Unsure how she'd react, I sat in silence. Suddenly, my mom ran out of the room, and then moments later, ran back in—holding a silk flower, as well as a photo. In that moment, I realized that my mom was wearing all black. She explained that she had just returned home from the funeral of her longtime friend. We stared at each other. My mother hadn't told anyone that she was going to her friend's funeral, let alone that she had been given a flower as she left, along with a note that said, "Thank you for your friendship." I described the woman as having a raspy voice and short brown hair, and there vanished any skepticism my mom could have had. Though my mother didn't understand how I was able to know what I knew, the undoubtable message from her friend gave her a visible sense of comfort. She didn't have to understand my ability in order to get closure from it. Besides, for what I was going through, there *was* no explanation.

Not understanding this part of myself didn't stop me from asking questions, and it still doesn't today. I found that from every question answered, countless more seemed to spring, and trying to figure it all out consciously proved to be futile. I was going to have these flashes of insight whether I understood them or not, and I couldn't help but become fascinated by what each sign and symbol meant, especially when they would reoccur.

My struggles during dream time became ones I would later face in waking life. The difference is, when the daytime visions come, there is no waking up. I had to learn how to maintain my composure when a wave of visions hits. At first, it was difficult to hide my reactions to what I was seeing. Luckily, being young, no one gave my occasional spacey moments too much thought. I never learned how to tune out the flow of information, but I did figure out how to keep it on the mental back burner. That way, I could concentrate on whatever was happening in my day-to-day life without too much distraction, in most cases. As you'd probably expect, it wasn't necessarily a graceful process—there were many times throughout middle school that I'd be talking to someone and completely lose my train of thought. I would be intensely focused on what I was seeing *about* the person, rather than what they were saying. I'm sure I came off as a bit of an airhead.

At the same time, the visions were unavoidable, and exploring their meanings was irresistible. Interpreting them became a passion for me, and I worked at it whenever possible. I filled journals with the symbols and visions I'd see daily. It was at this time in my life that a turning point occurred: I went from receiving messages randomly to learning how to initiate communication. Mastering how to be "on cue" was one of the most useful lessons of my life. It got me in the habit of consciously opening up, tuning in, and delivering information. It also caused me to become quickly aware of the hidden parts of people I didn't always expect. By that, I mean all of my relationships ultimately became affected by my gift. I found myself trusting my visions and instincts more than the words people told me. This led to many disappointing hunches that proved to be accurate, time and time again, no matter how much I gave people the benefit of the doubt. I was used to being on the receiving end of skepticism, and now I had become skeptical of other people. As I matured, I gradually grew out of my cynical frustration, but it foreshadowed an internal conflict that would always come with the territory. What do I trust more: other people's words or my own intuition? Not an easy question, when it comes to those you love.

As I hit my teens, I was going through all of the normal teenage trials of passage, but with an added sense of angst and alienation. Even though I felt so different, I tried to be cognizant of the fact that we were *all* learning who we were as people. I wasn't the only one going through radical changes. This was a commonality that certain open-minded friends felt they could share with me, and I always appreciated it.

One of these friends was Nolan, a small, shy boy who was in my physical education class. More than anything, we bonded over our mutual passion for computer games—but then again, we were thirteen. As time went on, I decided to reveal my secret to him. I described the other side of reality, into which I had been having glimpses for the past three years. To his credit, he didn't freak out. Rather, being technically minded, Nolan found my "weirdness" fascinating and was determined to give it a name. He would be instrumental in helping me research, through books and websites, what it meant to be a *clairvoyant medium*. When I first read the definitions of various forms of empathy, I felt like I was reading a symptom list of my entire life. We spent hours at libraries and in front of computer screens, reading the stories of others who had experienced similar phe-nomena. With this research came the startling realization that there *were* others. As you might expect, my interests expanded to include religion and spirituality—two subjects that are obviously connected to communicating with the dead, yet to which I hadn't given much thought.

Despite finding a name for my ability, I found myself unable to relate to many of the other subjects with which mediumship seemed to be lumped together. I cringed at the sight of the words *paranormal, supernatural,* and my least favorite: *occult.* My natural state of being was my "normal," my "natural," and it certainly wasn't shrouded in the secrecy implied by the word *occult.* I was immersed in a world that both united and divided me—now I knew what I was, and I also knew what I wasn't. I found the gimmicks that come with New Age spiritualism to be off-putting, and I hoped, even in those early years, that I could somehow help redefine what this extra sense is all about.

I immersed myself in all types of theology and ideologies. I attended a Presbyterian church for nearly a year, began reading heavily about Buddhism, and started trying to open my mind to philosophy and alternative ways of thinking. I didn't know what to believe—a lot of different philosophies could support the otherworldly visions I was experiencing. I knew undoubtedly that life continues on beyond death, and that it is clearly a state of existence that can interact with ours. Beyond that, I was open to many, if not all, possibilities. I checked out books from the library on religion and philosophy, spending entire summer vacations reading and trying to retain as much as I could.

Still, it was impossible to figure out where exactly I fit in. My search took me many places, and I figured that if anyone would know the definitive answers to life beyond death, it would be others with my ability. I set my sights on finding other mediums, determined to find someone like me who could provide answers to my list of questions, which grew by the day. At first, the only mediums I knew of were famous—John Edward and James van Praagh were two immensely helpful sources. They paved the way to the world of modern mediumship. I read their books, watched their readings, and saved money in the hopes of seeing them in person. I scoured the Internet and spiritual bookstores, looking for someone who could give me a live, in-person reading, but had little success at the time.

It was through this research that I acquired a significant understanding of what I was going through. I learned what it means to get feedback from others (validation), as a way to minimize the period in which I hold on to the impressions. This was a pivotal moment, because I went from being an open receptacle for any energy around me to someone who could at least control the duration of the experience, by either sharing what I was feeling, or not. Usually, upon sharing it, the vision or sensation would go away—relief that was immediate, but short-lived, until another message took its place.

One of the few people I was comfortable getting validation from was Nolan. We tried multiple "tests" to understand the capability and extent of this unique part of myself. We would loiter around parks and coffee shops, reading, writing, and exploring the depth of my ability. I wasn't nearly polished enough to invoke it on a whim, but through practice, I got better at homing in on individuals. This became an essential skill in my work. At first, our experiments were fun and sort of reckless—I'd read people in public, write down my impressions, and sometimes even walk up to people and ask if they were open to hearing any potential messages from loved ones coming through. During this turning point, I went from being a passive recipient of my gift, to starting to tap into its deeper potential.

Initially, walking up to total strangers was awkward, and the reactions were mixed. But the more comfortable I became receiving and delivering connections, the more messages came through. As the months passed, the subjects of these impressions began shifting. As opposed to just getting brief flashes of a deceased grandmother, the first initial of a name, or a sentimental memory, I began getting direct impressions from the *living* people I was reading. Relationship problems, health matters, and career changes all began coming through in my readings. Even more bizarre was the amount of trivial information I'd receive—random colors, seemingly unimportant memories, and a lot of what seemed like informational noise. Through practice and trial and error, I learned to navigate the impressions and get validation on the most important messages, while being able to partially ignore information that didn't seem relevant.

This put me in a position that presented challenges. Who

was I to say which message was important to deliver and which was not? Do mail carriers get to choose which letters they deliver? It didn't seem fair to censor, but I wasn't evolved enough to attribute meaning to the signs and symbols that were more ambiguous or that required more interpretation. Nolan was one of the few people who understood the benefits and downsides to feeling so much. During one of our first meetings, we walked the schoolyard as he told me about one of his close friends who lived a state away. As he spoke, the name "Jennifer" and the number "2" immediately flashed in my mind. To Nolan's surprise, the very friend he was discussing had two sisters, the youngest being Jennifer. As soon as I said the words out loud, the vision disappeared, and my mind went temporarily quiet. Whatever this ability was, it wasn't limited to space or time; I could read people through other people. Through intention alone, a connection could be made at will. As a thirteen-year-old, this ability felt like a superpower. It was a gift I wanted to develop; I just wished I had a mentor who could show me the way.

This period greatly defined how I'd step into my work as a medium, and much of what I do now was discovered then. While on the phone with a friend one day, I was doodling on a piece of scrap paper. I felt the pen glide back and forth, as waves of information began coming through. Sketching was a way I'd learned to channel information. I was initiating communication, as opposed to being at the mercy of dreams and random visions. At least in some way, scribbling allows me to exert a sense of control over the flow of what comes through. The resulting scribbles are generally meaningless. It's the actual process of scribbling that enables me to get into the meditative mindset required to initiate conscious communication.

Discovering my abilities was exciting, but there were definitely days I wished I were normal. Having nurturing people around me made all the difference, but it didn't make seeing vivid premonitions any less jolting. In at least one case, it proved traumatic.

My oldest childhood friend was nearly my carbon copy in appearance, but he was much more outgoing. We were more like brothers than friends, so watching Tim struggle through childhood brain cancer affected me deeply as a child. With treatment after treatment, the radiation that destroyed his vocal cords ultimately put his cancer in remission. I always felt that our bond was unique, because we both understood what it meant to be close to the other side, though in two different ways. Tim understood from an early age just how valuable life was, and he had a zest for everyday things that made him a joy to be around. He didn't view me as Tyler the medium. He simply valued my personality and friendship. At this age, I'd become pretty obsessed with understanding my gift, but Tim's situation reminded me to be present in the moment. We spent hours riding bikes, going to the beach, and inventing games.

In my mid-teens, my family moved nearly two hundred

miles away from Tim's family, but I still visited him on the weekends when I could. After a couple of months of not seeing him, my dad surprised me with an impromptu trip to the coast to visit my best friend. It was a beautiful day for the beach, and I was excited to go biking. As I walked to meet Tim on the pier, I could see his smile. I heard his gentle, shaky voice yelling out my name from afar. When I got close enough to hug him, I was anticipating warmth, but was met with a cold chill. He was laughing and smiling, yet as we embraced, I was overcome with noises of beeping and flatlining, loud in my ears. From deep inside me, a drain into emptiness; a precognitive vision of my best friend's death. There was no question, no room for symbolic interpretation, just a cold truth I wasn't at all ready to face at such a young age. I wasn't able to hide that something was seriously wrong. Unsure of what to say, I told him I wasn't feeling well, and I cut our trip short.

Had I known that would be our last interaction, I like to think I would have done things differently. But back then, unable to cope with what I had seen and what I knew was coming, I progressively lost touch with my best friend until three weeks before his death, at the age of seventeen. The cancer came back quietly, but more insidiously than it had begun. Three weeks before his death, Tim reached out to me and asked to see me for the last time in the physical world. Though he had just reached early adulthood, his life was ending. We agreed to go on a short road trip, to make up for lost time.

The trip never came. Tim's condition escalated to the point at which he was immobile. Before long, I learned that hundreds of miles away, my best friend had taken his final breath. I had no forewarning of the exact moment. It was a sobering reminder that, though I'm a medium, I'm also subject to the mysteries of the universe, just like everybody else. I was angry and frustrated. I didn't know what to do. I found myself praying for guidance from a God I had no name for or understanding of—I just hoped *someone* was listening. I knew that, at the very least, Tim was listening. In the days following his death, my prayers were answered in a series of dreams in which he, healthy and happy, met me on the pier where we'd shared so many earthly memories. He exclaimed in a voice that was clear and undamaged that he had "made it."

I think that Tim understood why I had withdrawn from him: I couldn't handle the burden of knowing. Still, I grieved. It seemed such a shame to die so young. I had missed so many chances to make new memories together. As this experience would foreshadow, the lines between my ability and my identity had blurred. Every personal interaction I had would be influenced by an additional, and not always welcome, second sight. Though I was gaining confidence in my ability to connect, I was feeling increasingly alone.

In the years that followed, I may have reached a deeper understanding of myself, but the life I was thrown into is always a series of question marks. When my mind is inundated with impressions that reflect the lives and feelings of the people around me, finding a sense of my own identity is a challenge. Despite my internal struggle, I find each reading gives me a deeper understanding of those who cross my path, and, ultimately, of my role. I think I had defined myself by this role, because it was the closest thing to a sense of individual identity that I ever felt. When I would share my ability with those who needed it most, I defined myself by my ability to help them. For better or for worse, it made me a perfectionist. Through trial and error, I was determined to refine my ability. Being a medium isn't a job I applied for—it's a responsibility that has added an extra helping of weirdness to the universal ups and downs of adolescence and young adulthood.

Hearing the profound messages of the dead has shaped how I view my own life. I learn from their mistakes, find comfort in their wisdom, and appreciate how drastically death affects the way we view life. As a young adult just beginning to navigate my own life, these lessons have been especially impactful.

2

Coming Out: The Psychic Closet

Downtown Hanford, California, was a sleepy row of abandoned brick buildings and family-owned stores that came and went, but essentially sold the same things— knickknacks, antiques, and an impressive variety of religious relics. About thirty miles south of Fresno in the central valley, Hanford was a quiet place to grow up with a strong conservative community. Imagine my intrigue when, one day, in one of the storefront windows, there appeared a new sign: GIFTS FOR THE SOUL. A large, happy Buddha statue smiled out from the window.

No one had seen anything like this in my neighborhood before.

I'll never forget my first time walking through the doorway, greeted by the sound of chimes and bells, and the odor that landed somewhere between patchouli and must. The entrance was flanked by Zen fountains and dusty bamboo plants. To the right was a table with colorful tapestries, ornate gems, and crystals, all without price tags. To the left was a closed door with a reflective finish. At the counter, was no one.

I walked around, examining things: tarot cards, chakra posters, faerie figurines, caged finches, and rows of meditation CDs in jewel cases. I would later learn that in the small room upstairs, belly-dancing classes were taught by the in-store tarot reader, and a wide range of alternative healing services were offered. It seemed that there was something for everyone. Books on all types of alternative healing and belief systems lined the shelves. (Yet in all of the times I would come to visit this store, the books rarely seemed to have been disturbed from their places. It was kind of the elephant in the room: in our provincial town, there wasn't much interest in "alternative" belief systems—or people, for that matter.)

Eventually, a tall, lanky man with wiry hair came out from the back of the shop. He introduced himself as Mark. Eventually, Mark and I would become friends. He was very talkative and happy to share his enthusiasm with anyone who would listen. He told me that he and his wife had opened the shop to create a space where people could come for "healing resources." I was nervous and unsure how much of myself to share, so I only acknowledged that I was in school with the hopes of becoming a nurse, and I had recently become more interested in spirituality.

Mark began to read out loud their newsletter, which listed upcoming store events—mostly meet-ups involving self-help and meditation. He practically breezed past the mention of a weekly Psychic Development Circle and something called "Mediumship 101." It was clear to me that he wasn't very interested in that particular subject matter, but my ears perked right up. Later, I became braver and began to test the waters. I inquired here and there about his thoughts on these subjects. I listened objectively as he discussed his ideas about everything from philosophy to the afterlife. Eventually, I would come to rent a room from him, in what would be my first formal reading space.

I'm so grateful to Mark and his store. It was the closest thing I had to a spiritual sanctuary. However, there were aspects to the culture that clashed with how I felt authentically spiritually minded people would behave. It was supposed to be a place for people of all walks of life, but there were still cliques among those who shared specific interests and beliefs. The paranormal investigative groups banded together, never mixing with the yoga-mat-toting moms who took weekly kundalini classes upstairs. These groups were really dismissive of each other, and there seemed to be little cross-interaction. The exception was the practitioners who did readings. The store revealed to me something like the underside of a leaf: the town's vital, hidden networks. And they were thriving! With dozens of fliers and business cards available at the counter, one could meet with intuitive practitioners or attend self-help groups nearly any day of the week. I began to meet people and investigate the various offerings, and before long, my head was spinning. Auras? Chakras? Reiki? I kept an open mind, but all of the new exposure just kept leading me back to one fundamental question: What did *I* believe?

This was a question I'd ask myself regularly, a sort of mental check-in when encountering different belief systems. I found that I resonated with parts of many beliefs, but I connected less with sources and practitioners that claimed absolutes. I noticed similarities between some elements of the store's culture and the church to which I had recently eased up on attending. Certain things did not resonate with me, whether it was intolerant Bible quotes or the Law of Attraction. Like any belief system, the New Age movement attracted a range of personalities, most of whom are well-meaning and searching for a deeper understanding about their roles in the universe.

The store became a sanctuary for *alternative* people, and I certainly fell into that category. I began to spend more and more time there. I'd study at the store before school and return there on my free time. I know that to much of the town, Gifts for the Soul was the kind of quirky place people gawked at from the outside, but never wanted to step into. To me, it felt like a home.

Though I wasn't keen to tell Mark of my interest in mediumship, I had no problem finding others who had tons of opinions about it. There were even a few who said they could receive information intuitively, as well. I was absolutely fascinated by the unique processes each of these individuals employed. Though all claimed to connect to the same source, the ways they went about it were just as individual as the practitioners themselves. There were various degrees of credibility, of course. This fact frustrated me deeply, but I was soon able to determine when someone wasn't being honest.

My search for guidance in my gift became a search to be understood, and it wasn't an easy quest. Over time, I did get to meet many people of varying backgrounds who possessed a second sight—some had it their entire lives, others were like me and found it after a life event, like the loss of a loved one or a near-death experience. Whether they worked in a neon-lit storefront or were internationally acclaimed, I found all of the mediums completely fascinating. Each had an inherently different approach to receiving the same information. I struggled to resonate with those who strayed away from the details and validation. Airy-faerie ambiguity accompanied with general statements weren't uncommon to see, but even those questionable mediums were intriguing in that they displayed to me how *not* to approach my readings of my own.

Most readers seemed to fall into two categories: those who focused on people's personal lives (future planning, counseling) and those who intuited philosophical or "big-picture" sermons to their clients. The detailed readers who emphasized validation were generally my preference to be read by, but I found that the more philosophically based readers also had something useful to give. The two types served entirely different purposes: one type for personal-life development and forecasting, and the other for a more broad-viewed, universal approach. There was one particularly memorable reading I'll never forget that sent me in an entirely different direction in my search for guidance—guidance that ultimately came from within.

I met a medium named Michelle. She worked out of the room with the reflective door near the entrance of the shop, and I asked to have a reading. Even before Michelle began, I could see in her eyes that her heart was in the right place. She had a kind voice, and the way she spoke, the time she took, and her utter sincerity convinced me that she wasn't fishing for information. She truly was trying to interpret something.

Initially, the reading was off to a vague start. She mentioned a vision of a chair and a ring. I had seen a lot of psychics by this point, and I didn't want to waste anyone's time with nonspecifics that could apply to anyone in *some* way. I wanted to validate. As the hour ticked on, at some point about midway through, Michelle kept mentioning that I had "guides" on the other side that helped me communicate with spirits. She described them as multiple beings—a team that would help me conduct readings and provide guidance, if I knew how to listen. It all sounded great to me, but with little other validating information, I took it into quiet consideration. Michelle told me that the best way to connect to my guides was through a process of meditation, something she was willing to teach me. Her timing was really interesting, as I had set up a meditation space in my room only a few days before, stocked with candles and incense. Just that morning, I had brought home a small aloe vera plant and placed it in the center of the room. As you can imagine, I was floored when Michelle told me, nonchalantly, that the guides were "showing me a plant . . . like a cactus." Here, she paused. "I see you meditating around it. Is this aloe?"

My jaw dropped. This was the validation I'd been looking for! There's no way this medium could have known such a specific detail about something I'd only just bought that morning. Since this vision was indeed correct, then maybe there was something to her claim that I had spirit guides on the other side. I felt like my meeting with this woman was meant to be—maybe my guides had sent someone to help me notice them. But who were they?

As I headed home, I was determined to meditate and have a word with these guides. Ironically, being determined is the exact opposite of how I would later, more fluidly, connect. The purpose of meditation, after all, is to *un-think*. To minimize thoughts and feelings, so as to be an unobstructed conduit through which information flows. Consciously trying to connect only takes me out of my intuitive perceptions and puts stress on the process, limiting the flow of information. But whatever, I was determined to try.

Arriving home, I put on some quiet background music, lit a stick of incense, and sat on the floor cross-legged, unsure of what I expected to happen. After a while, I realized how counterproductive it was to consciously un-think. So instead, I let go. I focused on my breathing. Nothing happened.

I took a short break. When I came back, I set a timer and meditated for a half hour more. Still nothing. I was frustrated, but I continued to meditate for the next few days, with little success in connecting, other than the usual back-burner impressions. I felt guided to communicate with my guides, but I wasn't hearing back from them.

After weeks of unsuccessful attempts at getting some personal guidance of my own, I was feeling defeated. I was confused as to why my spiritual guides weren't coming through with the clarity with which other people's departed loved ones so often did. Why were my guides, who were meant to help me, heard from the least?

After many daily attempts at connecting to my guides, I decided to let them come to me. By this point, my nights were filled with vivid dreams, consistent visitations, and a blur of ever-shifting perspectives. While still learning to hone my waking ability, I made it my goal to improve dream-time communication by trying to remember the most relevant pieces of information and disregarding what seemed like noise.

As I was in the midst of refining this process, I was shocked when after months of nearly nightly visitations, they suddenly came to an abrupt stop. Instead, repetitive dreams of being submerged underwater seemed to take the place of all the dreams I was usually able to remember—psychic or not. The first few nights, this timeless, formless dream was oddly soothing. Though I was lucid, a feeling of being immersed in warm water was a nice relief from the nightly bombardment of connections that were often draining.

This state had a sense of distant familiarity, like a memory to which my subconscious was on the verge of alerting me. As seemingly peaceful as this dream began, there was a feeling of unease in the womblike realm that made my heart race.

After each night that passed, I'd awaken in the morning recalling an additional detail with every repetition of the dream. As the week went on, my recurring dreams were gradually evolving into a series of nightmares. By the end of the third week, insomnia had set in. I struggled to sleep for long periods of time, because I frequently woke up to take a break from sleeping. What do you do when rest itself becomes exhausting?

The usual line of spirits that had come through nightly was a different kind of tiring. They were, at least, familiar and comfortable. Anything was better than the new spinning, suffocating heaviness that besieged my mind. Dozing off, I felt the usual warmth of slipping underwater and the sense of vertigo that had been increasing over time.

Then, out of nowhere, a *tug*. The vertigo was interrupted by a physical pull on my left arm, which startled me as the spinning came to an abrupt halt. Still immersed in an ocean and unable to see, I heard a voice say directly, "You don't remember this, I gave you a hand."

I was baffled, but also relieved to hear another person. The voice didn't seem to have a source, but it sounded like a young man. There was a feeling of familiarity that seemed to radiate to the core of my soul—I felt like I'd known that voice for longer than I'd known *anyone* in my present lifetime. It was like recognizing someone I couldn't quite put the name to.

"Walter," the voice said. "That's who you knew me as."

I wanted to engage this strange-yet-familiar presence, but as I floated aimlessly, I was unable to speak. Though the sickening vertigo had ceased, I was too afraid to open my mouth and risk the sensation of water filling my lungs. Everything inside me fought the urge to speak—a battle I lost. My lips parted, and what seemed like an ocean's worth of pressure rushed in. Jolting awake, I gasped for air. When I got up to wake my mom, she said I looked very pale and offered me a glass of water. As politely as I could manage, I declined.

When I told my mom about the series of suffocating nightmares, I could see the concern in her face. Though she was always willing to patiently hear about situations that she couldn't begin to relate to, I knew she didn't understand how much these dreams affected me. I hoped that if I shared with her what this Walter person had said, maybe she'd be able to fill in the blanks, and the nightmares would cease.

Logically, she suggested that my dream could be about a previous scary experience involving water. She reminded me of an incident during a Hawaiian vacation we took when I was a small child. My dad and I went out to explore tide pools, since I was too young to snorkel. With our backs to the ocean, a six-foot wall of water rose up behind us and threw us onto the sharp, volcanic rocks beneath our feet. According to my mom, she watched helplessly as the waves nearly washed me out to sea—a fate that they later learned had befallen another swimmer that same day, at the same beach, with a tragic result.

I was completely baffled as to why I hadn't remembered my childhood near-death experience, and why it was just now manifesting in my dreams. When I pried my dad for more information about the incident, he told me that it was a sore, traumatic subject that he never intended to bring up.

In a split second, he had relied on the current of the water to nudge my body within his reach, allowing him to grab my left arm and pull me toward the shore. I began wondering if Walter had somehow intervened, helping give me the nudge toward safety—and saving my life as a result.

Getting these answers from my parents was a step in the right direction, but they opened up a lot more questions. If Walter was watching over me as a small child, long before I'd lost anyone I knew, then who exactly was he? And if he wasn't anyone I knew in this lifetime, then why was he helping me at all?

The repeating nightmare never came back again. Like the impressions that stay with me until interpreted and delivered, this nightmare dissipated as soon as I understood its meaning. Walter—whoever he was—introduced himself into my life by showing me how he saved it.

The nightmares stopped, but my visitations with Walter continued off and on, often with complex symbolism and imagery that came through while I dreamed. I began to realize that Walter's insight into my life—his awareness of it—reflected that he knew much more about me than I knew about him, which was practically nothing. Though I didn't always see his face in the dreams in which he'd visit, his presence became an easily recognizable feeling.

The more I noticed the signs and synchronicities he'd send, the more would follow, in rapid succession. I couldn't help but wonder how much control these guides had in directing my life—and how did they benefit from guiding me?

As I would later learn, every single soul is interconnected, but some have more prominent roles in the lives of others to help teach certain "soul lessons." These teaching-oriented relationships are sometimes referred to as soul contracts, and they can exist in multiple forms (more on that later). Many of our soul contracts are with people who serve a profound purpose in helping us understand what it means to be human, while we're living a human experience.

In some cases, soul contracts aren't limited to just *living* people. These connections can—and often do—exist with our spirit guides. Depending on what lessons both souls are learning, they take on roles that will allow for opportunities to learn them.

It's important to note that the roles of spiritual guides are—like all roles—temporary. After all, change is essential to growth. The souls of guides continue on, just as ours do, and they have their own unique lessons and challenges before them. Regardless of the role a soul takes on during any one incarnation, in this realm or another, all are temporary roles that shift and evolve.

Walter presented himself differently, depending on the situation he was assisting. If I was needing comfort, he'd come in a dream in the form of a compassionate, human-looking friend. If a message was particularly serious, he'd devote his energy to showing me solutions, with only his familiar feeling to reveal himself as the source. Coming through in dreams was ideal, as it allowed for clear communication without the biases that come with being conscious. Yet the more I paid attention to being open and receptive, the more I began seeing undeniable signs in waking life.

Through documenting my hunches, random recurring thoughts, and occasional daydreams, I realized these were all means of communication from my guides. For me personally, meditation in the traditional sense wasn't essential to "hear" them. Through trial and error, I learned how to interpret symbolic information. I'd spend an hour a day meditating, with little success in bringing through much of anything. Then I'd go out in public and find myself interacting with my environment and having space-out moments in which something specific nearly always came through.

One of the most profound examples happened in my mid-teens, when my mom and I decided to grab dinner at a local pizza parlor. From the moment I walked in, my eyes were drawn to an empty high table that stood beneath a beer sign. Strangely, my intuition seemed to be getting a "ping" in the same general direction, with no origin in sight. Every time I looked at it, I felt a sense of urgency well up inside me, as though I'd forgotten something incredibly important but couldn't place what it was. This feeling was the definition of distracting, but no matter how hard I tried, I couldn't shake it. I was unsure of even how to describe what I was experiencing, although I had proven myself to my mom enough by this point to know she would probably understand, to the best of her ability.

As I tried to ignore the dimly lit sitting area (and contemplated getting our food to go), the two men in front of us placed their orders and went to find a seat. As they walked through the parlor, I saw one of the men walk up to the empty table that had been demanding my attention. In that minute, the deep sense of urgency I'd been feeling amped up to a new level, now paired with rapid mental flashes in succession of a lanky young man wearing 1980s-era clothing, then an old car racing down a street, and then out of nowhere: the taste of metal in my mouth.

A stranger might never have guessed what was happening to

me, but my mother knew me well enough to tell. She could see that with each vision, my body tensed with chills that came in visible waves, the hairs on my arm standing on end.

"Tyler, are you getting something? Tell me!" she insisted.

As I tried my best to articulate what I was feeling, describing more and more as each image rushed in, I saw her face change. Tears began to well in my mom's eyes; the hairs on her arms now visibly stood, too. She now looked nearly as overwhelmed as I felt.

"That man, sitting beneath the sign, is someone I went to school with," she said. "His brother was killed in a car accident, in his twenties."

At this point, neither of us was sure of what to do. My mom encouraged me to walk up to the guy, but something told me not to. Here I was, in this random pizza place, completely immersed in a scene only feet in front of me, receiving a reading for a total stranger. But I ate my pizza and pretended it wasn't happening, until the feeling went away. Deep within, I felt that somehow this was a lesson that showed me the importance of using discernment with whom I share a reading. If someone is in too vulnerable a headspace, then having a loved one come through can be detrimental to their grief process. I may not be in control of the information I receive, but I *am* responsible for how I handle what comes through.

I wish I could say that after a while, my guides came and did a meet-and-greet. The reality is, their messages and influences have proven to be as elusive as they are profound. For years, I tried to put faces and names to my guides—to humanize them and to try to get some explanations. Since then, I've come to believe that there are simply things that I'm not meant to know. Without a doubt, my "team" is greatly helpful in the communication process, and they guide me throughout my life—even if I'm not always consciously aware of it. The forces behind my ability are just as much of a mystery to me as they are to others. One thing I do know for sure is that each message is brought into my life for a reason, and it's my purpose to fulfill that need.

It was in that moment—with my mom, at the restaurant—that I remember a conscious shift. My guides were around, and though their contact was subtle, I always seemed to notice it when I was supposed to. After not approaching the man at the table, but still getting the validation of the vision's accuracy from my mother, I felt compelled to find people who wanted to hear the messages I received. I was determined to start reading people in a more refined manner. I knew that I received information essentially two ways:

1. By reading life-events/information directly from the client's energy. When it comes to understanding how a client feels about a situation, or looking into the most intimate aspects of their personal lives, the best source is often the client himself. When I look into the past, present, or future of an individual's relationships, health, and personal fulfillment, I'm generally doing so by reading that person's energy, which retains their experiences and is leading them down a particular path. If a person is too deep in grief, unwell, or putting up walls, then this method of reading can be less reliable.

2. By reading information/getting messages from a spirit. Spirits that come through and share messages give insight from *their* perspective—which is the whole point. However, given that what I present as "information" is reliant on what they communicate, I have to trust that what's being communicated is the entire truth. Additionally, given that their language is often one of symbols and images, information can get lost in translation, if a medium isn't careful.

I was coming to understand that the best readings were a bit of both of the methods listed above. I believed that a truly competent medium could navigate intuitively reading the client's energy, while simultaneously interpreting information from their guides and loved ones. Being able to have more than one way to intuit information is important, in the event that one method is blocked or inaccessible. Integrating both methods makes for an overall stronger reading from multiple perspectives. Though this was the goal, I didn't have any formal experience doing readings, and I wasn't sure what refining this practice would look like. For the questions I had, I knew that the shop was my answer. In order to expand on what I did naturally, I had to put myself out there. Working at the shop was the most logical (and intuitive!) next step. To do so, I had to get Mark's permission to do readings.

This was obviously a concern, because I'd avoided sharing the medium side of myself in our *many* conversations about that very topic. To do so casually, after such a long period, might make me look deceptive, which, of course, I had been. A few days later, I walked into the shop the minute it opened. I was hoping to talk to Mark, and as usual, he was the first one in. I didn't have much experience explaining my situation. I was still very shy at that age, and I stumbled over my words as I described that first moment of connection after my grandmother's passing. Mark nodded silently when I said I wanted to do readings out of the side room. I could feel his eyes on me as I spoke, but I couldn't get a read on what he was thinking. In a sense, I suppose this was my first job interview!

Mark asked me to perform a reading on the spot, to see if I could "pick up on anything" other than a whiff of skepticism. After all, he wanted to make sure someone working out of his store was credible. We made our way into the side room. We sat at a table, and I relayed the details of the process that would ensue. As I explained that I often hold on to personal objects to help establish a connection with a specific loved one, he stopped me midsentence and asked, "Does a photograph of the person I'm wanting to connect with work, or does it have to be an object of theirs?"

Immediately, I could tell he didn't have such an object. This is a hurdle I would have to overcome in many future readings, and in this moment, I was mortified to think that I might not be able to connect. Spirits seem to come through, in part, based on the intention of the living to communicate with them. The more open a person is, the more likely they are to be receptive to a "spiritual experience." By bringing an object belonging to a specific loved one, the querent is thinking about the person with whom they want to connect every time they look at the object. In a reading, which can easily distract a client with information overload, holding the object helps both me and the querent stay focused.

As I sat with my hands folded and my eyes shut, Mark waited. I focused on my breathing and took the leap of faith that something would happen. Initially, nothing. I flashed back to scenes of Nolan and me practicing psychometry exercises, in which I'd close my eyes and he'd drop an antique into my hands, held behind my back. In this exercise, the objective would be to give details about the object—the era of its creation, where it was from, or who had owned it. In hindsight, our teenage hobbies were a little weird.

After a few moments, the darkness behind my eyelids shifted into a bright red numeral "2," and then a piece of torn lace. I knew, thanks to experiences from other readings, that torn lace was my personal symbol for divorce. I spoke up about two prior marriages, and Mark acknowledged he had been married twice. Next, I saw a blue numeral "3," which shifted into a man that looked nearly identical to Mark, except his nose was red and blotchy. These symbols weren't as clear-cut as his ex-wives, so I had to describe what I was seeing with as little personal bias as possible. After doing so, Mark validated that this man was his brother—an alcoholic who, at the present moment, was at the bottom of his addiction. He also happened to be one of three brothers.

At this point, I was clearly reading into matters in Mark's life that were weighing heavily on his mind. In just a few brief visions, I felt like I knew more about what mattered to him than he had ever divulged in the entire time we knew each other. Clearly affected, Mark shifted in his seat. I described the family dynamics that played out, due to his alcoholic brother's self-destructive behavior. Mark wasn't expecting so few images to symbolize so much about the relevant issues—and neither was I! I was feeling self-satisfied to have overcome the hurdle of being deprived of a focus object, but then I saw that Mark had become visibly vulnerable. He had all the proof he needed to have me work there, and that was the limit to which he was ready to delve into a reading—for now.

With the reading having been cut short, I was just happy to have proven myself. Ironically, I still couldn't really get a clear read of how Mark felt about me. After a few awkward moments of silence, Mark agreed to let me rent the room under two conditions: I had to charge money and give the store 25 percent of my fee, and as a minor, I had to get full permission from both my parents. Initially, I wasn't sure which was more mortifying: the prospect of charging for readings or asking my conservative dad if I could employ my ability to speak with the dead—an ability he didn't even know existed. But, I had to give it a try.

First, I went to my mom. I asked her opinion about working openly as a medium and, more pressingly, how to discuss it with my dad. I knew that the demands on me would require serious thought. To make matters more complicated, for as long as I could remember, I had always felt that if someone charged for their gift, they ran the risk of losing it. I had never read professionally, or even consistently. I had a lot to learn. My mom, supportive from the start, said she would encourage whatever would make me happy.

That left only my dad. I was even more nervous talking to him than I'd been pitching to Mark—at least Mark was expected to be open-minded, because he ran a store devoted to alternative thinking. My dad, not so much. Anxious for him to come home from work, I scribbled out my case in the form of bullet points on a notepad. I practiced my speech in the mirror. My parents had always said I would have made a good lawyer, and I was about to put their claim to the test. However, no amount of preparation could have readied me for his reaction. His face shifted from confusion to incredulity to what looked like . . . pity? His response: "Absolutely not."

That was a tough day. It's one thing for a parent not to support your professional dreams, but a medium is who I *am*. This was my calling, and now I could not pursue the only avenue I knew. I probably should have brought it up with my father sooner, but I had feared his reaction. And now my fears had just been confirmed.

I went into my room and threw away any reminder of the shop and anything I'd bought there (remember, I was a dramatic teenager). To me, it wasn't just stuff. It was all part of my journey of self-discovery as a person. Though I wasn't sure how much I believed in chakras, my Hinduism books reminded me that there were other ways of thinking, beyond the rigid beliefs I encountered at school. It freed me from the restraints of the fear-based mentality so prevalent in our community. Now all of it sat in the middle of the room, crumpled in a heap that I never cared to see again.

After that, I was depressed. I didn't speak to my dad much. I hurt deeply for many reasons, but the biggest was that he was missing out on such a large part of who I was. It wasn't just that I couldn't share my gift with others who came to the shop—he wasn't even open to having it shared with *him*. How could we be so deeply disconnected?

My dad, of course, noticed my behavior. Eventually, he brought up the subject again, more gently this time. I continued to build my case. Ultimately, after many discussions, explanations, and demonstrations of my sincerity, my dad came around. He didn't understand it at first, but he proved that his love for me surpassed everything else. Loving me for me ultimately meant accepting my ability (even if it took endless tests and questions). His permission elated me, but he did reiterate that he was still concerned about how I would be received by the people in our community. And truthfully, so was I.

I did readings out of the shop for the next few months, in what would prove to be one of the most transformative times of my life. Though my family encouraged and supported my decision to work openly, there was no way to predict how any one person would react or how they'd fit into my life. At one of my first formal readings at the shop, a short, older gentleman in his mid-sixties had strolled through the shop. He seemed out of place, but when he saw me, his eyes lit up. It was as though he recognized exactly who he was looking for. I got a feeling like I was meant to play a role in this person's life. We're all given signs like this now and again—déjà vu is just one of them. The man approached me, said hello, and asked if we could step into the small space where I did readings. His energy was kind and paternal. Somehow, he was significant.

He told me he needed a reading, and he agreed to the basic rate the store charged for us to rent the space. As we sat across from each other, I was anxious. I was still new to professional readings, and the large number of practice readings I had done had mostly been for women. Where I was from, men were far less conversational about alternative spirituality (though I still got a lot of wives asking for readings on their husbands' behalf!). The man who sat in front of me didn't seem to be reserved in that way. He radiated sincere, excitable interest.

I started by explaining that throughout our session, I preferred he tell me as little about himself as possible. It was important for me to intuitively feel my way through the course of the hour, unbiased. That meant keeping validation to a yes or no, and saving elaboration until after the reading was over. As I eased myself into the reading, I slowed my mind, focused on my breath, and closed my eyes.

The first thing I heard was chirping, followed by the crashing of palm trees—perhaps in a storm? Shades of vivid green replaced the darkness, illuminating my field of vision, though my eyes were still squeezed shut. Briefly, a tan dot within a flutter of green came more clearly into focus, revealing a man dressed in tribal garb—meaning, very little at all. His eyes spoke to his age, and his mouth was a straight crease. He looked right at me.

Just as I was beginning to process these details, they faded into darkness. I fought the urge to feel frustrated. I never seemed to be able to control the length of the visions. Even today, depending on the skill of the communicator, some visions are so quick that I miss them, and others go on for what feels like forever. I've learned to process details quickly and make every second count. In this reading, after only a brief moment, I opened my eyes to see my customer still sitting across from me, waiting expectantly. His expression was one I'd come to see a lot in my line of work—a look of hope. He was looking for a specific message that could answer whatever profoundly intricate problems he had.

Composing myself as best I could, I explained to this stranger—whom I'd met only moments earlier—that I had just seen a vision of a half-naked man in a jungle. While I was expecting laughter or derision, instead I saw tears. Trembling, this man who clearly carried himself with a lot of self-respect released what looked like many years' worth of pent-up emotion. He acknowledged that the person I'd described had monumental importance to him. He was an unlikely loved one: his shaman.

The man explained that in his spiritual search, he had traveled throughout South America and studied extensively with medicine men and native elders. One such elder was the man who appeared to me, who had passed only a few months before. Though this was the only major vision to come through, it was deeply meaningful for this man. He felt a reconnection with his mentor and guiding light. For me, it was reassuring to see that no matter what the man had come in expecting—and no matter what was left still unanswered—I could give him this. It was proof beyond a doubt that their relationship continued even beyond death. It eased the weight of a lot of pressing questions, for both of us.

As the man and I said our goodbyes, I was struck with a strong sense of familiarity. I wondered if it was my guides telling me there was something to learn here. It would be one of many readings in which I felt like both the teacher *and* the student.

Only a few months later, I encountered the man again. Though I was starting to do more readings out of the shop, I'd also recently decided to take a safer, more practical route for my life. I enrolled in pre-nursing classes at the local college. The day I registered, I was surprised to run into this same man. It turns out that he was the soon-to-be-retiring dean of the college. He remembered me from the reading, of course, and said he was surprised that I was pursuing nursing. With a gift like mine, why wasn't I working as a medium, full-time?

We talked for a while, and though I went through with my plan and signed up for courses, I came home feeling like that day was meant to be. For all my eagerness to begin college— I knew I'd learn a lot, meet new people, and possibly find a career—intuitively, I felt more excited about something *else*. It was certainly validating to hear the same sentiment from a man who clearly saw the value of education, who'd made it his life's work. What I took away from our second meeting was the idea that, for me, perhaps nursing wasn't meant to be. At the time, I was nervous to even take this idea into consideration. If I pursued hospice nursing, I could make a good living as a caregiver, use my gift on occasion, and still have relative anonymity. If I worked as a medium, and if I was actually successful (a big "if"), it might be much harder to live a quiet life.

Taking the synchronicities as the signs they were, I decided to test the limits of my ability. If this was something I was seriously meant to do, I wanted to see how thin I could be spread. I would gauge the range of my exhaustion levels and better understand how to pace myself in the future. I decided to see how the locals would react to a free group reading, one night per month. It would be an opportunity to hone my skills, I thought, and to get feedback and validation from others. I also wanted to open up the experience to those who might be skeptical, or nervous about meeting me one-on-one. On the first night, I invited my dad to come watch.

Expecting about thirty attendees, we set up the upstairs room with as many chairs as we could. We were surprised by how quickly they filled up. My mom and I awaited my dad's arrival. Then, among the sea of unrecognizable people streaming in, a familiar face walked through the door—not my father, but my first grade teacher, Mrs. Whitmore. She immediately recognized me and embraced me in a hug. I remembered her as a stern woman who occasionally scolded me for not paying attention. I was shocked to see her here, now, in this crowd, looking older and far less intimidating than I remembered. She said she had been walking down the street and had noticed the crowd lining up on the sidewalk, waiting for the event. By now, many people around town knew about the part of myself that I had long kept secret, and she was no exception. In fact, she could hardly hide her curiosity.

"Tyler, do you get any impressions off me?" she asked, point-blank.

I wanted to oblige, but I was distracted. I was focused on the fact that I was about to do a massive group reading, in my hometown, for the first time ever. On the other hand, this was my old teacher, and I wanted to please her. I suggested we walk over to a more private area.

I ushered her into the small side room, where we sat quietly for a few moments. It felt awkward showing this deeply personal side of myself to someone who was once an authority figure, but she was clearly open and eager to hear what I had to say. Perhaps there was a reason she had happened to walk by the shop that day.

I closed my eyes and took a few deep breaths. As I sat quietly, trying to connect, no clear impressions came. My anxiety that I wouldn't pick up on anything began to overwhelm my thoughts. How would I explain this, with more than one hundred people outside the room waiting for a group reading? The more analyzing I did, the more panicked I became. I could feel her eyes watching me from across the table, waiting. What if tonight was a complete failure? The impressions usually came so naturally. In this moment, I was feeling as disconnected as I had ever felt. Mental chatter and anxiety only make the process of un-thinking more difficult. This was a dynamic I would have to learn to navigate throughout my entire career. To meet the expectations of a reading, it was essential to detach from the expectation of an outcome. As the minutes merged into a continuous awkward silence, my internal freak-out was interrupted by a voice that boomed from across the table.

"Stop overthinking! This is serious," she said. With my eyes still closed, I flinched at the prospect that my teacher was scolding me—*during her reading*. I whispered that I needed a moment to collect myself. A completely different person's voice said, "Take your time, the silence is peaceful." I opened my eyes, shocked, as cold chills shot down my spine and along my arms. I had no visuals, no images at all, but my gaze and my teacher's locked. I heard the second voice again, saying clear as day: "My granddaughter has uterine cancer. This is an emergency."

The clarity of the message astounded me. This second voice belonged to someone only *I* was hearing, presumably my teacher's grandmother. It had never happened like this before, and never with such force. Flustered and unprepared to deliver such a direct message, all I could muster was that I felt that my teacher should go to a gynecologist. Her brow furrowed as she responded, "Are you sure? I just had an appointment recently. I got a bill of clean health." Now I felt even more awkward than before. I knew what I heard, but this was sensitive stuff. I did what I could, which was to encourage her to get a second opinion. The voice that came in so clear never came through again.

Feeling discouraged, I explained that I wasn't getting anything additional. She seemed disappointed. I hadn't met her expectations of what she was hoping to hear. I was starting to learn that disappointment sometimes comes with the territory of being a vessel: I have no control over what comes through, only how I choose to deliver it.

As I shuffled out of the room and into the storefront, all eyes were on me. The chairs were full, with many people standing in the back. More attendees lined up at the door, all hoping for a connection. Some came with objects that belonged to deceased family members. Others came with living family members, in hopes of creating a stronger connection. The excitement that buzzed in the cramped room proved to be more burdening than invigorating. For the first time in my life, I was scared that I wouldn't be able to correctly interpret the messages on such a large scale. To make matters worse, by now my dad had arrived to watch. I could see him sitting near the back with my mom. If this went south, I had to see all of these people around town, at school, and in the community. And so did my dad. There was no running away.

I had no idea where to start. Swallowing my panic, I couldn't shake the feeling that I wasn't prepared for what I was walking into. Yet the minute I began explaining to the audience how I go through my process of reading, a miracle happened. Multiple people started coming through, clearly and concisely. It was as though someone had suddenly flipped a switch. My mind cleared, and I spoke for five hours. I read more than sixty of the hundred people who came to the event. The hours flew by, as I read for one person after another. This was something I'd learn about the process, when applied on a large scale: I'd be so focused on delivering the messages that once the information was shared, I was on to the next person. I couldn't give much thought to the repercussions of what I was saying. My parents watched from the audience, but I paid little mind to their reactions. I couldn't have focused on them, even if I wanted to. Conducting readings meant sharing my headspace with the many individuals who came through, and I lost all awareness of my surroundings. In one instance, an elderly woman's sister came through as a child. She told me that she had died in a tragic horse accident. Before I could communicate this fact, my attention was brought to a man who sat in the back row, stoic and tight-lipped. As I focused on this man, a whole group of father figures came through, acknowledging that they had all suffered heart conditions. All of them wanted me to mention the man's own susceptibility. As I rambled on without any visible validation from him, his wife interrupted. "He's had multiple heart surgeries," she said. "And heart conditions run in his family. He's just not speaking up!"

The man smiled sheepishly, making it clear that he understood what I was saying. I continued delivering messages. As the night went on, people came and went throughout the store. It was one of the most popular events the venue ever had. Regardless of Mark's opinions on mediumship, he was clearly happy that people were crowding in. Afterward, people gushed to him about their experiences. Though his pleasure was palpable, all I could feel was relief that my first group reading had been a success. That, and utter exhaustion!

My parents had left midway through the event. When I arrived home later that night, I found them sitting on the couch, waiting for me. My dad had tears in his eyes, as he told me how overwhelmed he'd been by the response I'd gotten. People had come up to him, asking countless questions—questions he'd never even thought to ask me. For the first time, he saw the healing that these readings could offer. It touched him that people were leaving with a true belief, and personal evidence, that their loved ones did indeed communicate through the person he knew only as his son. From that day forward, my parents became supportive of my career and life purpose to the absolute fullest. Overnight, I went from feeling fundamentally outcast and misunderstood, to having a more honest and open relationship with my parents about who I was. The part of me that seemed to garner so much attention—that I'd struggled to manage—was now the pride of the family.

Nearly a year after that first event, my phone rang. Not recognizing the number on the screen, I almost didn't answer. On the last ring before it went to voice mail, I picked up. I heard a voice that sounded vaguely familiar. The woman on the other end was the teacher I had read on the night of the group reading. She was calling to tell me that shortly after her reading, she went home and told her family about what I had said. Though she personally had no interest in getting a second opinion, her family urged her to go anyway. What could it hurt? She called to tell me that if she had not gotten that second opinion, her stage 3 uterine cancer might not have been caught in time. After extensive treatments, she told me that she was on the road to recovery. She said my reading had helped save her life. I replied, "Thank your grandmother—she's the one who told me!"

That monumental validation would be one of many profound instances of medical information that would come through in readings. It is a special skill I didn't yet understand, but I also didn't feel I needed to understand it. It was enough to know I could be of help. After the readings, people began contacting me in droves through word of mouth. In my overzealousness, I often did up to eight consecutive readings a day. These hourlong sessions took so much mental energy that I felt constantly exhausted and drained. I continued to push my limits, testing the boundaries of what I was capable of, in the name of better understanding the scope of this sixth sense.

Eventually, I would learn to pace myself. But for now, with my parents' full support and a community that was growing to accept my unique ability, I felt I was living my purpose—for the first time in my life, and in a very public way. Little did I know just how public it would become!

3

Near-Death, Near Life

Shortly after my eighteenth birthday, I was at one of the most volatile moments in my career. In two short years, I'd gone from doing readings in the small town of Hanford to being driven to Los Angeles nearly every weekend to meet clients. While my career was booming, my parents' business was at its all-time low. No matter how resiliently my dad showed up to work every day, family finances ultimately required my mom to get a part-time job. This meant that for the first time in my life, my mom would be working outside of our home, and I'd be seeing her much less. On some level, the timing seemed to be sending a message: I was a legal adult and therefore had to take on more responsibilities.

But nothing could have prepared me for the unique responsibilities that came with being a medium. One of them was to share the impressions I was given, even in situations that could be complicated to navigate. This was a dynamic that affected my relationship with my parents. Though they were supportive, they still didn't understand the *how* behind what I was able to do. Sometimes I'd see impressions about my parents and their personal histories, which by default was a little awkward, since they were my parents. I could navigate a little embarrassment here and there, but what I wasn't prepared for was what played out one morning when I was jolted awake with a feeling about the man who raised my mother.

Though he was known to be in good health, my mom mentioned one morning that my grandfather had a slight cough. For whatever reason, I couldn't seem to move past the fact that my generally healthy grandfather was feeling a little under the weather. As I feigned interest in the rest of my mom's conversation, I couldn't shake a feeling of an increasing tightness in my chest. This was different, though, than the feeling I get that indicates lung cancer. This felt more similar to the asthma I had struggled with as a child, but different. Allergies? No. Something felt off.

As I told my mom to call her dad and urge him to go to the doctor, I was more disturbed by how I was feeling emotionally than I was physically. The chest pain was undeniable, but the emotional response that welled from my gut didn't match the level of a cough. It was as though part of me was reacting to news I hadn't received. But how? And if what I was experiencing was real, my biggest question was, *why*?

That night, I went to bed upset. Almost more frustratingly, I didn't understand why I was feeling so bad. Waves of emotion seemed to ebb and flow, imprinting on my mind. Knowing of impending tragedy was a challenge in itself, but not knowing the full span of what was about to happen was even worse. Knowing partially was more of a burden than not knowing at all.

Part of me knew, but not all of me knew. The signs were there, but I didn't want to believe what they were showing me. The next morning, I woke up feeling the same undulating pressure with which I had reluctantly gone to sleep. In that moment, I woke with the all-too-familiar feeling of a memory that hadn't happened yet: my grandfather had seven more days on earth.

At this point, I was shocked with how eerily history seemed to be repeating itself, nearly a decade later, with my grandfather. Except now, I was given more time to deliver the message. Why was I always the one to deliver the bad news? More important, could knowing in advance help me prevent my grandfather's death?

Understandably, this was a message my mom took hard. In a surreal moment the next day, I stumbled into the kitchen to get breakfast and told her that somehow, I knew her father had exactly seven days to live. Absolutely shocking, considering that morning he had called feeling much better. After the number of readings I'd done, I came to trust my intuition before trusting the way any situation *seemed* to be going.

As difficult as telling my mom was, it proved to be one of the most beneficial messages I could have ever delivered. In a matter of days, what started as a light cough spread into an immobilizing lung disease. By day four, my grandfather had been admitted to the hospital.

Even then, I don't think anyone expected him to pass with the same conviction that I did. I knew it had everything to do with the fact that this was a prospect that was too difficult to accept. After all, he'd been healthy for as long as anyone ever knew him. Why would that change now?

But it did. By the sixth day, he had lapsed into unconsciousness and was being kept alive through a respirator. In less than a week, my mom went from chatting with my grandfather at his home to having to say goodbye at his hospital bedside. To make matters even more difficult, she was left with having to make the decision to either keep him alive or take him off the machines that kept his vitals going. I was reminded of one of the earliest insights I'd ever been given from my guides: being on life support is like wearing locked handcuffs.

My mom chose to set her father free. On the seventh day, he took his final breath. My mom derived a sense of comfort from having known a week in advance that her closest father figure would pass. From her perspective, his death was fated and unavoidable. Knowing beforehand bought her the time to say goodbye in the best manner possible. In a universal irony, just as I was realizing how oblivious my grandfather was to his serious health problems, I was utterly ignorant of my own.

As we went through the deeply emotional process of losing

a loved one, all of our attention was on him. Meanwhile, my mom juggled her job and the legal responsibilities that came with her father's death, all while grieving. The whole family was massively distracted. Far down my priority list was the subtle, reoccurring headache that throbbed from behind my right eye. What's a headache when you're dealing with so much?

One event that has a way of shifting your priorities is being told that you may die imminently. As I lay in bed in the ICU, I thought about how strange it was that only twenty-four hours earlier, I was working in my garden after jogging two miles. Now nurses told me that I was not permitted to move, let alone walk, at the risk of my brain rupturing.

What started as a dull headache quickly developed into something more serious. Initially, everyone around me rationalized it as an allergy headache, and understandably so, considering it was the earliest days of spring and I spent hours outside working in the family garden when I wasn't doing readings. It had become something of a meditation spot for me, surrounded by nature and in contact with the earth. It was one of the few places where my ever-racing mind found tranquility.

As the days went on and the pain intensified, peace of mind became harder to find. Within the first couple of days, I visited my local optometrist. He did a full assessment of my eyes and told me there was nothing visibly wrong. I was likely just dealing with seasonal headaches. Within forty-eight hours, I was dealing with a radiating heat that pulsed from the crown of my head to my spine. My mom took time off work and drove me into town to see the chiropractor. He performed an adjustment on my neck, saying that my back was the likely cause of the seemingly random pain. Despite the number of differing opinions I was getting, I couldn't help but think back to three weeks before the pain started. I was with my mother in the car, asking questions about my difficult, premature birth. In passing, she mentioned a brief incident when I was a baby, in which she was told I may have suffered a brain aneurysm. At birth, a neonatal scan showed a potential bleed at the base of my brain. After a second scan was taken, she was told that the first must have been a mistake, and the doctors weren't concerned about it. This was the first time I had ever heard the story, and from that moment on, I couldn't shake the feeling that somehow that dot on the scan would come back to haunt me. My mom repeated that there was no way it could ever be an issue, because it was simply a technical error.

"I think we might see it again," I blurted out as my mom drove.

"Ty, don't say stuff like that, you're being a hypochondriac," she said. Reliving the fear of losing her only child was too much to bear.

Yet, relive it she would—as predicted—three weeks later. As I stumbled into the ER, my face was going numb, and I was struggling to get my words out. We had assumed we were going in to get a migraine diagnosis and medication to ease my pain.

My mom was met with a rude awakening when the first nurse to hear my symptoms rushed to fetch two other doctors. They said I needed to get a spinal tap urgently to test for meningitis, a fast-acting cause of death in young people. While the doctors discussed this among themselves, I knew from the core of my being that I did not have meningitis—and getting a spinal tap would waste what little time I had left.

To the dismay of my doctors, I flatly refused to get a spinal tap. I insisted that I get a CAT scan on the base of my brain. After multiple arguments, it was clear that everyone was frustrated with me and thought I was being reckless. "*We're* the trained professionals," a nurse protested, summing up what everyone around me was feeling.

Finally, a CAT scan was ordered with the agreement that if it came back clear, I'd submit to the spinal tap. But that needle in the back never came. A new doctor rushed into my room with the news that brought my mom to her knees. Doctors often word things in the most unsettling of ways. This one said, "It's never good when you're the most interesting case in the emergency room. Today, you're that case." He continued: "You have a mass near your brain stem, and we need to transfer you. But I'm more concerned about the fact that your brain is swelling."

My mom collapsed, hyperventilating, and had to leave the room. I was wheeled into an ambulance and transferred an hour away, so that an MRI could be done to establish the severity of the brain mass and the swelling. After having been poked and prodded with a wooden stick on my face, hands, and feet, another disturbing revelation was presented: I was showing symptoms of a small stroke. All of this information was unloaded on me over the course of ten minutes, and for some reason, I wasn't even remotely scared yet. I just wanted to be fixed. Knowing that I had potentially suffered a stroke wasn't what bothered me. The unsettling part was not knowing what the grape-size mass on my brain stem was. No one else seemed to know, either. Any attempt at getting information out of anyone was met with general statements about needing to be patient and wait for the recommended treatment—be it chemotherapy if it was malignant, or simple brain surgery (!) if it was benign. What had started as a dull ache a week earlier had morphed into icepick-through-the-eye pain that reflected what was happening internally: my brain was swelling up against my skull.

The official diagnosis was hydrocephalus, due to a benign arachnoid cyst that had blocked the ventricles of my brain from allowing cerebrospinal fluid to flow properly. This caused swelling, partial paralysis, and a number of other issues that would manifest in the following days. Emergency brain surgery was ordered to aspirate the cyst, allowing the fluid to flow properly. My brain was swelling in its own fluids, obstructed by a mass that I had been born with (but was only now symptomatic). That entire first night was spent trying not to move so much as a millimeter—and wondering how all this happened so quickly.

Nothing prepares you for the very real prospect of dying young. People sometimes talk about how they'd react in such situations, including me. But the reality is that it's impossible to tell how you will react, until it happens to you. In my case, I was calm about it. I knew that overreacting wouldn't do any good, and the last thing I needed to do was stress my brain even more. To make matters worse, I was also having my first exposure to being in an ICU ward since discovering my ability. As hospitals are some of the most spiritually active places, I avoided them for years. People always assume that graveyards are full of ghosts, but the reality is, souls tend to stick around familiar areas. People often spend their last months in hospitals, and if they're unable to transition fully, they naturally stay in those areas. Though the physical body may reside in a cemetery, the consciousness that once occupied it has no connection to the cemetery as a place.

The first night in the ICU was the most difficult, by far. I was woken up hourly by a doctor who would ask me the same general questions and do a basic mobility test, which I later found out was to ensure I wasn't lapsing into a coma. The debilitating headache that made all light and sound nauseating was only slightly numbed by the medication, making real sleep impossible. As I drifted in and out of consciousness throughout the night, I couldn't help but notice that every so often, I'd see a man standing beyond the window in my door, in the darkness of the hallway. The first time, I paid the distant observer little mind, assuming he was either a nurse or a patient. As the night crept into the early morning, I would only see him every few hours, and I'd go through two or three hourly checks with no sign of the man in the distance.

As the early morning dragged on, my exhaustion was beginning to peak. Not only was I tired from the interrupted sleep, due to the hourly check-ups, but the pain that had started as a dull ache was now an exhausting agony that made every inch of my face hurt. What was unforgettable in that daze was the man who reappeared through the window, closer to it now, this time with a single hand pressed against it. In the haze of my mind, the darkened silhouette that now seemed much closer still wasn't any more recognizable, which I knew, even in my altered state, wasn't normal.

Within forty-eight hours, my condition had worsened to the point that an emergency plan of action was established: the surgeon was to go in with a drill-size incision to drain the blockage that was stopping my fluid from flowing properly. Being that the mass itself was so close to my brain stem, extra caution had to be exercised to ensure that the surgery went as planned. As the hours dragged on, I lost my sense of night and day. My only chronological milestones were my hourly wake-ups and sight-ings of the mysterious visitor that only I seemed to notice. Even in this state, visions and impressions came through in waves. The exact specifics of each vision seemed to come and go, but one thing was for certain: regardless of how I was feeling, spirits were going to try to come through. I was noticing the man with his hand at the window more and more frequently, but I found comfort in the fact that he never proceeded past the threshold.

By the morning of the surgery, I was nearly incapable of lifting my arm, let alone asking questions about the man at the window. Shortly before going into surgery, I remember in one of my waking moments a series of visions, "downloaded" in rapid succession. First, I received a viewpoint from the top of the hospital. I was surprised to see bright flashes of light reflecting off rain puddles, considering that California was experiencing a drought and it had been sunny when I was admitted. The second impression came in the form of a sound—a loud drill that buzzed like a dentist's. In a split second, I felt my consciousness shift to the viewpoint of the man at the window. From his perspective, I could see my thin body entangled in wires and surrounded by monitors. Though I knew this was me, it felt deeply foreign. I was most taken aback by a sense of my body's deeply depleted energy. I saw a life-force that was running out.

I would later learn that many people who deal with potentially life-threatening situations report being visited by people on the other side, be it family or people with whom they're not familiar. Oftentimes, as people get closer to transitioning, their capability to connect to the other side is enhanced, as is the capability of those on the other side to reach us. Time and again, spirits will acknowledge that they did not go alone—there was always someone there to aid them in their transition. The man at the window may have been waiting to aid me in my transition, if my condition continued to worsen. As my health declined, he drew nearer to the glass between us, until finally he was close enough to touch it.

My blood pressure began dropping rapidly, sounding alarms from the monitoring machines, with no help in sight. In this moment, something deep inside me changed. All fear left me. I was holding on no longer. I didn't want to die at eighteen and leave the beautiful life with which I had been blessed, but at the same time, I knew I had no control and simply stopped fighting. As my heart began slowing, I remember asking my guides, "Why are you taking me now?" No response came.

Soon after, I went into emergency surgery to have the cyst aspirated. I don't remember much from the point at which my blood pressure dropped to the surgery itself. I didn't pray, I didn't say goodbye to anyone or have any last words, I just existed in the moment. I didn't mind. Nothing seemed urgent or dramatic. Death didn't feel like an ending; it just felt like life would go on. No words can truly describe that contented feeling. Everything else seemed insignificant. It was all going to be okay.

Despite letting go, I was jolted awake. I was alive. My first feeling was relief, as the relentlessly skull-crushing pain was noticeably absent. In what felt like seconds, I had undergone a successful six-hour brain surgery (and they didn't even have to shave my head!).

While I stayed in the ICU, I rarely encountered other patients. The reason was that almost everyone there was unconscious, due to either illness or sedation. Even considering the bad shape I was in, seeing people in far worse condition was a reminder of how lucky I had been. I was by far the healthiest patient in the ICU. More than that, I knew I was going to be able to go home. Many who shared the same hospital floor didn't have the privilege of knowing that, or even hoping for it. One night, I was awoken by the howling screams of a woman. Her loved one, who I assumed was her son, was being wheeled in by a group of medical personnel rushing down the hall. Not much older than me, this young man had been shot in—as I would later overhear from the night-shift nurses—a gang-related incident. Tragically, life support was his only option. Throughout the duration of my hospital stay, his family waited in the lobby with my parents.

When my mom visited during the hours she was allowed, we spoke about the young man whose condition far exceeded mine. In a strange way, discussing his state helped me disconnect from my own. As updates of his condition worsened, I couldn't help but wonder when he was going to make his transition. Apparently, the family had to make the decision to take their son off life support, accepting that he would pass naturally as soon as he was no longer artificially assisted. As I spoke to my mom about the tragic decision his family had to make, I felt guilty for having complained about what I was going through. My mom went home at the end of the day, but I couldn't help but stay awake throughout the entire night.

Something deep inside told me that I would have a second chance at life. As I was wheeled through the hall, past the now-empty hospital room, I knew that the other young man on my floor didn't have the same chance that I did. I was released from the hospital on a rainy morning. Life seemed to be restarting for me in countless ways. Most obviously, it was continuing on without the only man I ever knew as my grandfather. The universe seemed to be sending me a lot of messages in a short period, all of which aided my search for perspective.

Only months before, I had just begun to deal with mourning the death of Tim. His face flashed in my mind as my parents huddled around my brain scans, searching for answers. I am severely claustrophobic, but as I was rolled into the MRI machine, I could almost hear his voice telling me that there was nothing to be afraid of. The fear I had experienced by not knowing what to expect in the next moment—that was Tim's *entire lifetime*. That, in itself, gave me a lifetime's worth of perspective.

On an even deeper level, my near-death experience validated the path I was on. If there was any way I could help bring closure to the woman who had to watch her son die, then that was truly living with purpose. I saw my own parents process the prospect of having to say goodbye to me. Seeing that, I felt like I got as close to death as one could get, without actually dying—a feat I had mistakenly thought was already covered by the fact that people on the other side communicated with me. I believe the congenital brain cyst grew to its obstructive size at just the right time to aid me in my search for perspective. Moving forward, I gained a clearer understanding of what the people who communicated with me went through before their transition. Even more significant, I saw firsthand how people handle the prospect of loss, death, and the grief process. In nearly dying, I was able to gain a deeper understanding of life and its continuation.

4

Hanford to Hollywood

As my number of readings increased through the years, it became apparent that I had to make a choice about what to do with my life and future. What had started off as a part-time passion, which I pursued when I wasn't going to school, became an opportunity for a full-time career. There didn't seem to be enough hours in a day to manage going to classes and doing readings in between. As hard as I tried, this was an unsustainable balancing act that wasn't meant to be. Still, working as a full-time medium was a massive leap, and it came with profound issues.

By this point, I had become very familiar with well-established mediums. I saw the lifestyle and the challenges that came with it. I knew my abilities were up to par, and I was already confident that I could perform large group readings and make fluid connections, even with the stress of doing so in a crowd. But this career path is unique. It comes with obligations and expectations unlike any other industry. For one thing, it exposes you to all kinds of public opinions, good and bad. Success in the medium world means building a career from press, visibility, and exposure—and, by definition, scrutiny. Whereas John Edward does his readings with a stern insistence on validation, I questioned whether I could be so self-assured as to navigate readings that gracefully. To anyone else in my position, going to school, getting a normal job, and living a quiet life of doing readings on the side would have been the most sensible step.

But I knew that this ability wasn't meant for shunting to the side. What I didn't know was that I'd become a whole lot less shy in a very short period—purely out of necessity. At the time, outside of my readings, there was no real need to be vocal. I showed up to my college classes every other day, took notes, and rarely asked questions during the lecture. It wasn't because I didn't have questions; I just never felt the time was right to speak up. This was an old habit from high school. It stemmed directly from the bullying I had experienced back then, which had left me somewhat traumatized—as I think it would for anyone. I was still coming to terms with those experiences and struggling with self-esteem issues, which contributed to me feeling so conflicted about the future. It wasn't that hospice nursing wouldn't be fulfilling. After all, I was surrounded by students and would-be nurses who showed immense passion, dedication, and a sincere calling to the career.

It just didn't feel like *my* calling.

I wasn't oblivious to the irony—while I had such remarkable insight into the lives of others, I felt entirely void of perspective for myself. I was being hired by adults three times my age to deliver guidance, but I struggled to find direction in my own life. It was a frustrating juxtaposition. In a room full of newly enrolled college students, I was hardly alone in my yearning for life guidance. This angst wasn't just a psychic problem, it was universal, but I had the additional burden of being expected to *have all the answers.*

We were all scared to commit, to choose a major that would lead to a lifelong occupation. What if we chose wrong? That stress alone is enough to make even the smartest of us question our choices. For me, the internal struggle became harder to navigate, as the combination of school and readings took up nearly every hour of my day. Realistically, I knew that maintaining this balancing act would ultimately negatively impact either my grades or my readings. But I wasn't ready to give up, either—or to make an immediate decision.

I'd attempt to study in between readings, and I'd find myself responding to emails from clients during class, as opposed to taking notes. Nearly every hour that I wasn't in school was spent either doing readings or thinking about them. As one solution to the increased number of requests, I'd even contemplated getting a secretary to help with scheduling. Taking the leap of employing someone was a big responsibility, and it meant that I'd have to trust someone with a task I myself struggled to do effectively. All of the buzz about my work was completely word of mouth, yet somehow, people from all around the world emailed requests for readings. Some came with in-depth stories of loss and desperation; others asked only when and how we could meet. To my surprise, I'd regularly find that people would include photos of their loved ones, and beg for a reading to validate that they were at peace in the afterlife. This constant barrage of tragic stories and desperate pleas became difficult to handle. It seemed that for every piece of correspondence I responded to, two took its place, and I felt guilty for not being able to respond to every grieving person.

Regardless, I did my best. My mom and I commuted regularly to Southern California on the weekends, so that I could do readings for L.A. clients. Even though my sixteenth birthday had come and gone, I had no interest in getting my driver's license. Initially, it was out of convenience, as my mom and I enjoyed spending the time together. But as time went on, I found that intuitive visions and feelings would come through on the drive to the reading. I knew that if I drove myself to readings, I ran the risk of being distracted. That wouldn't be good for the client, and it would be even worse for the other drivers on the road!

On one weekend trip to L.A., a talent manager I had been introduced to invited me to a talent search. Initially, the idea was entirely out of left field. I knew I wasn't destined to be an actor. I was still on the soft-spoken side, and my singing ability was strictly limited to the shower. Showcasing my ability on a stage in front of an audience of jaded Hollywood types didn't feel like my cup of tea. I preferred doing readings privately. Besides, I'd be the only medium in a sea of more typical creative talent—would I be laughed right off the stage?

When I woke up the morning of the event, something deep inside me urged me to go, just to give it a shot. The feeling was strong enough to overcome my fear and shyness. Somehow, I knew I was meant to be there. I swallowed my doubt and walked through the entrance of the cramped theater, adding my name to the audition list. There were about sixty seats visible in the dim lighting, and to my surprise (and chagrin), almost every one was filled with an agent or manager, all of them holding clipboards and making notes on each performer.

As I sat in the back corner, I watched as one actress after another took the stage to perform her monologue. Aspiring musicians, child actors, and poets all presented the best of their talents in what they clearly felt was a make-it-or-break-it moment—their big chance to be seen by an agent who could change their lives forever. I admired their passion, but I didn't share it. Frankly, I was just looking forward to the event being over. I didn't have a need for an agent, and a full-time manager seemed like overkill. All I really needed was someone to help with scheduling.

At most, I thought I could use the opportunity to prove myself to an audience of people who intimidated me. After all, these were skeptics. They were probably bored and expecting to be disappointed, as opposed to the enthusiastic patrons I was used to at the shop. I knew I often learned the most when I took risks. When it was my turn, I summoned all my confidence and walked onto the stage. Lights shined in my eyes, making it difficult to see the audience. I heard quiet murmuring. Already, this felt very different from what I was used to.

"My name is Tyler Henry, and I'm from Hanford, California," I said. "And I'm a medium." From a dark corner of the audience, a man's voice called out, "Why do we care about your shirt size?"

I laughed off the heckling. I explained that as a clairvoyant medium, I receive messages from spirits on the other side. Thankfully, one such message began coming through at that very moment. A flash of pink sparked from the darkness on the right side of the audience, which symbolized a female presence. As I nervously focused on this bread crumb of a lead, my mind filled with an unlikely image: the state of Virginia. I was never any good at geography, so it was a small miracle that I could identify it.

I called out into the audience and acknowledged that a strong mother figure was coming through, and that she was making a reference to "Virginia." Immediately, a husky-voiced southern woman called out from the audience. "My aunt's name is Virginia, and my momma passed." I found her in the audience, and when our eyes met, I was confident I was on the right track. Waiting for more flashes, I paced the stage nervously.

Distressingly, a feeling of pressure began welling beneath my sternum. My hand reflexively covered my chest. Trying to not look like I was about to jump out of my skin, I explained to the woman, "She's having me rub an area below my sternum, and she's bringing my attention to this area." I paused.

Next, I saw a ribbon flowing through my headspace, my symbol for cancer. Navigating carefully, I added, "She's framing this in the context of health, though. She's with you through this."

The woman's slow, bashful smile made her eyes crease. She pulled down the collar of her shirt, revealing a chemotherapy port. She explained it was to treat her stage 4 pancreatic cancer. With this single action, she had the entire crowd gasping and whispering among themselves.

More images began coming through, along with more questions from the audience. I was able to read several of the agents and managers with messages directly from their loved ones. Once the images picked up, I couldn't really process the impact of what was coming through. I could only deliver the messages to the best of my ability. Still, I imagine that if some of the more cynical agents might have been expecting a gimmick, they were quickly surprised. And yet, for the number of questions I was asked, no one expressed any interest in representation or management. They were just curious. All except for one: a tall, older man who sat in the back, watching silently.

I exited the stage and went through the back door. I was still processing what had just transpired, and my mind was buzzing with residual images. I'd been onstage for nearly an hour. I had managed to get their attention, yet none of the agents asked to speak with me afterward. I'm sure I was too far in left field for most of them to know what to do with me. They were used to actors. Most of the agents gave the impression that they didn't even take mediums seriously, at least until they'd seen me . . . "perform"? They didn't even have a word for what I did.

All, that is, except one. As I walked down the street to take a breather, I was met with the familiar face of the man who'd sat silently in the audience. Business card in hand, he introduced himself as Ron, a publicist and personal manager. He had represented a few professional psychics before, as well as a number of actors and musicians, throughout a forty-year career. He asked if I was interested in having a manager, and what my goals were for the long term.

I told him that I really only needed help with scheduling. Ron smiled. He said he could do that and more. He urged me to take a meeting with him, and before I knew it, Ron started introducing me to his friends and professional acquaintances. What started out as a single meeting became meetings every weekend, with Ron and someone new for me to read. With word of mouth spreading, my new manager not only helped alleviate the stress of scheduling, but also introduced me to people who would change my life in a miraculously short period of time.

In the first few weeks, I read a gamut of people, ranging from *Days of Our Lives* cast members to movie executives. I felt my shyness start to evaporate. When I'd confess to Ron that I was a little intimidated by these people, he'd remind me that many of them were intimidated by me! It was true that whether I was reading a wealthy studio head or a passionate young actor, they were all just humans wanting to connect. I got better not only at interpreting the messages but also at communicating them sensitively. For anyone who has experienced a loss, connecting with the other side can be deeply emotional, and many of these clients weren't used to feeling so vulnerable.

As demand grew in L.A., especially in Hollywood, I found comfort in returning home to Hanford to have essential downtime. Between work and study, it was nearly impossible to find time to decompress. I decided to take a semester off from school. Ron scheduled that time, and it filled up quickly. Before I knew it, I was doing anywhere from two to eight readings a day, ranging from forty-five to ninety minutes each. It was a ton of work, but I did enjoy getting to experience some fascinating environments, with people who were as unique as the lifestyles they led.

One such man was introduced to me at a Christmas party in Beverly Hills. Michael was a successful producer and television personality who had, serendipitously, been interested in working with a medium. All that was missing, he said, was the *right* medium. He suggested that we meet for a reading, and Ron scheduled him for the following weekend.

Initially, I had minimal expectations—when you work in Hollywood, you hear a lot about so-called opportunities. Yet when the day arrived, I did feel something auspicious in the air. Before seeing Michael, we had a meeting with another new client. As I walked up the stairs of the client's historic apartment building, I found myself in eerily familiar surroundings: standing on a massive checkerboard-tiled roof, with two pyramid structures at the perimeter. Chills ran up my back; this was more than déjà vu. Incredible as it sounds, I recognized these details from a reoccurring dream I'd had as a child. . . . I was sure I had stood on this very same checkerboard, between two pyramids. As a kid, I'd never remotely suspected the dream was intuitive. I have weird, nonsensical dreams just like everybody else—but the resemblance here was undeniable.

As I talked my way through it, my client interrupted me with a single word: "synchronicity."

It was an idea that was still pretty new to me, but the client was right—it described my situation pretty well. Synchronicities are events, similar to coincidences, that act as messages from a person's guides or loved ones. These seemingly random yet serendipitous moments are instrumental in changing the direction of a person's life forever. On the afternoon that I left the checkerboard rooftop to meet Michael, it was clear that there was something important going on.

My nana Barbara Koelewyn and me, when I was about six months old. It was her passing that triggered my first experience with "knowingness."

My beautiful parents, David and Theresa Koelewyn, and me, when I was about six months old.

Hanging out with my dad in the backyard, at about ten months old.

Here I am at three years old, near Yosemite National Park, on a fun adventure with my family.

My dad and I decorate our tree during the Christmas season, which was always a big deal at our house.

Enjoying a relaxing day at the beach with my mom. We lived in Cambria, California, a small seaside town, for a few years when I was growing up.

My family loved to spend time together by attending baseball games. I was about thirteen here.

My mom and me at our first "Hollywood Halloween Party." At just sixteen years old, I didn't know this would be the first of many to come!

Kendra Wilkinson was really fun and funny . . . that is, until I told her she's likely going to be a mom again!

One of the coolest settings we've shot at was Rob Dyrdek's Fantasy Factory. The two of us had a nice little argument over whether he was going to have a boy or a girl. I won! #congratsrob&bryiana

I can't say enough about Monica Potter. She is one of the kindest people I've ever read, and I was so happy to be able to bring her some closure after the loss of her dad.

Lil Jon expressed that he went from skeptic to believer during our session, but my favorite part was introducing him to my mom at the end of our reading!

Both of my readings with Nicole "Snooki" Polizzi were not only filled with much laughter but also incredible emotion. She's definitely a favorite.

Roselyn Sanchez's reading actually culminated with some "permission" from beyond to pursue her latest project.

Bringing Jennifer Esposito's dog Frankie through was so shocking and emotional, it even caught me off-guard.

Glee's Kevin McHale had a great energy, and we had such an interesting reading. I think he's got a little bit of clairvoyance in him, as well!

For a seventeen-year-old, singer Madison Beer has suffered some significant losses. It was great to be able to offer some comforting words.

Michael lived in a big house in Laurel Canyon. I was driven there and joined by Ron and my dad (who had accompanied me that day, so he could sit in for the business part of the meeting). I was proud of my dad for how far he'd come. He'd adjusted particularly well, considering it had only been a year since I went full throttle as a medium. He had to accept so much about his son, in a short period of time. I still wondered what he thought about all of it.

After a deeply emotional reading, Michael introduced us to his business partner. We all sat around a table to discuss some ideas for growing my business, including pitching a possible TV show. It might sound obvious now, but at the time, there was nothing like it on-air, and there hadn't been for many years. Michael and his partner described some ways we might move forward, including filming some of my private readings. In the biggest surprise of the day, my dad piped up. He confessed that he was curious to see some of these sessions, which he'd heard so much about. That meant so much to me!

Having everyone discuss my gift with such normalcy was an enormous relief, after years of repression. It's what I remember most about that day. When Michael suggested I do a large group reading at his home, full of "industry people" and friends, I didn't even blink. In just a few months, I had gone from zero to sixty. I found myself adjusting to a lifestyle drastically different than the one I came from.

That group reading took place a couple of weeks later. I had my parents drive me back up the winding hills to the secluded residences that overlooked Los Angeles. I remember I brought a notebook and wore a blazer that was a size too big. I tried to radiate confidence. The agreement was that I was to be separated from the other attendees, so that I would have no idea who I would be meeting or reading. By this point, I was used to being kept in the dark about my clients before a reading. It was something I requested. Not only did it ease people's skepticism (since I couldn't do any "research" on the attendees), but it also gave me an excuse to avoid making awkward small talk. I was socially anxious and didn't want to have to rub elbows with people before reading them. Plus, I wouldn't be biased with any preconceived notions about them, and I could more easily trust my intuitive feelings.

As Michael led me to the other wing of the residence, I was surprised to pass by such a large number of attendees—many more than I was expecting. There was a wide array of people— in age and, I assume, occupation—waiting to hear messages from beyond. I assumed they would also have varying degrees of belief, at least initially. As I explained my process, some listened intently while others seemed to check out, just wanting me to cut to the chase. Unfortunately, I couldn't do that even if I wanted to. Explaining my process is an essential part of connecting. After all, what good is it in delivering a message if the person receiving it doesn't understand the context in which it comes through? For this reason, I always make it a point to explain that my "sixth sense" works through the other five senses. I explain that I am a bit like an intuitive bloodhound: once I get what feels like a solid lead, I pursue it in the hopes that as I speak, additional sensations will materialize.

As my eyes scanned the audience, I tried to establish who would go first. The impressions came fast and furious. A vision of a grandmother with lung cancer pinged off one of the females in the front row. Just as quickly as I was thrown in that direction, the energy of a dog—specifically a pit bull—came through in a completely different direction (I get impressions from animals all the time!). Just a few seconds into the reading, and I was already overstimulated. I tried to calmly process each image, as I put the pieces together.

The grandmother with lung cancer connected to the woman in front of me, but no one claimed the pit bull for the ten minutes I spent obsessing about it. It wasn't exactly my choice— I felt really compelled to find the owner, plus I knew it was harder to receive new impressions until old ones were delivered. Usually, once I delivered a message for someone in the audience, that soul would free up my headspace for others to come through. (That's why, when you watch my readings, you'll notice that I focus far less on the information that makes sense to clients, and instead focus on what doesn't. I sometimes even encourage clients to talk to relatives for follow-up validation; these often end up being some of the most profound messages, once they've landed!)

I continued scanning the audience, and made my way over to a pretty brunette girl who had tears in her eyes, from watching the other readings. In a striking British accent, she introduced herself as Charlie.

Almost immediately, a woman I identified as Charlie's grandmother came through, painting for me the picture of a relationship that had ended abruptly, with some kind of personal trauma attached. Through symbols, her grandma acknowledged for me that a blood vessel had ruptured, and she made some sort of reference to her makeup. Strongest of all, I felt a deep sense of love for her granddaughter, which cut across all time and space. Charlie's emotion was palpable. She told us that she had watched her beloved grandma die unexpectedly in front of her, shortly after Charlie had a conversation about her makeup. The grandmother's spirit positively radiated with her granddaughter's validation, which made the message so fulfilling to deliver. Not only was her grandmother a beautiful communicator, but Charlie had an energy unlike anyone I had ever met. Just being around her, I'd later find, helped get me into a receptive, open mindset. Her spirit and way of thinking were like a powerhouse for spirituality . . . and ultimately made her a perfect fit as my future assistant, a role she would step into after a series of synchronicities of her own.

But that was still to come. Meantime, as the sweet grandmother's presence faded away, there were other messages to deliver. By the end of the three-hour group reading, I felt fulfilled, but absolutely exhausted. I'd brought through communications for more than thirty people. Yet it was the validation that came after the reading, from a young publicist who'd sat silently in the audience, that was the icing on the cake. At the end of the event, she pulled me aside to apologize for not validating during the group. Her pit bull had been put to sleep the day before, and it was still too painful for her to talk about. Obviously, I was relieved that the message had been valid, and I was pleased that the dog had finally made that connection with its owner. On the other hand, this was representative of an issue I'd face more often now that I was doing groups: not everyone was ready and willing to validate publicly. Each time I had insistent impressions that no one would claim in that moment, it left the audience confused. It also prevented me from freeing up headspace that could allow for additional messages to come through. But any job has its difficulties. I had to accept that I wouldn't always get validation, and figure out how to work around it.

In the following months, I continued to do group readings at Michael's home. Ultimately, these readings were filmed, as I proved myself to person after person. These videos were shared with the right people, and at the end of a monumental year, I received a phone call. A network wanted to film a reality television show that would document my life and work! If I was going to make a living as a medium, this was about as big an opportunity as I could ask for. Nothing could have prepared me for the incredible journey that would ensue, but I was as ready as I felt I could ever be!

I've always been confident that sharing my ability, to whatever place it may take me, is my soul's purpose. I've left all other paths behind to follow my passion, and so far, it has worked out perfectly. With one synchronicity after another, my intuition and my guides have always seemed to point me in the right direction. Of course, having the right people in my life has certainly been a contributing factor. My intuition has played a role there, too. I've been able to discern who is trustworthy, and who is not. When my life was changing in unpredictable directions, intuition was an internal compass I could rely on, no matter the situation. Outside of readings, I practiced trusting my intuition on a daily basis.

Frankly, these days I'm even a bit scared to deviate from what my intuition tells me. Any time I've gone against my gut, I feel like I've paid for it. My guides come through on their terms, not mine, and they have often guided me into humbling experiences that taught me vital lessons.

In one case, I arrived late to the train station on my commute back from L.A. and was shocked to see the line for the ticket counter extending out the door. I had ridden this particular train before, and though an eight-dollar ticket was mandatory, I had never seen any officials check passenger tickets in the countless trips I'd made previously. As I stepped over the threshold onto the crowded train, I had a vision of a ticket, with a section sign flashing overhead. Immediately, I felt my heart sink. My first instinct was to find out which section I was in, so I could make sure it wasn't the place where the vision indicated *something* about a ticket. I could still make it home, I thought, as long as I avoided the area in the image. Slowly pushing my way through the crowd to the nearest sign, I was mortified to realize that I had inadvertently walked *into* the premonition I had experienced only moments prior. Two stern cops and a police dog rushed into the train corridor. They loudly instructed everyone to take a seat, so that they could check everyone's ticket. For an eight-dollar mistake, I felt like I was in an episode of *Locked Up Abroad*. I was sweating profusely, awaiting my fate. When the older of the two officers came to my seat, I pulled out my wallet. Tucked inside, I had a ticket from a previous ride. With my hand shaking, I handed over the crumpled piece of paper. I wished I had hopped off the train at the first indication of potential concern. I couldn't help but hear "Told you so!" in my head as the officer inspected my ticket. Only feet away, I could hear the other officer reprimanding a ticketless passenger. Apparently, when they do check, they take it seriously! For some reason, the officer holding my old ticket didn't discern that my ticket wasn't valid. Lesson learned!

I took this experience as an indication from my guides to pay attention when visions that pertain to my life come through. I was confident when delivering my visions about others, but when it came to myself, I was still a stubborn teenager who sometimes had to learn the hard way. Regardless of what I saw, it was only as helpful as my willingness to heed the warnings.

These warnings—and a keen intuition—would be essential as I made the move from my small town to the big city. We had been commuting to L.A. off and on to meet the demand, but I still had a lot to learn about my newfound home. On my move-in day, my family and I had to bring my belongings from my childhood home to the new apartment. As we hurtled down the highway, I was dozing off in the front seat, as my mother drove.

As I sat resting my eyes, I was at the border of sleep when I felt the distinct need for our car to switch into the far right lane. Still startled from having dozed off, I promptly instructed my mom to get into the other lane immediately, and that I'd explain after she safely moved the vehicle. Ultimately, no explanation was required—my family watched a wooden table fly off the top of the car that carried it, directly in front of us. When my mom switched lanes, she narrowly missed the table that would have certainly gone through the windshield of our car. To this day, my family tells this story as a reminder of the importance of going with your gut—going with mine narrowly avoided disaster for all of us.

For the amount of times where intuition came in handy, adjusting to L.A. life certainly had its fair share of mishaps. I came to a lot of realizations the first week of living solo. Not having my mom around to help out made me realize just how incompetent I was at navigating the dishwasher. On one of my first nights alone, I decided to order a late-night pizza to celebrate my newfound independence. After waiting anxiously for forty-five minutes, I opened my front door and stepped out to take a peek down the hall to see if hope was in sight. That's when I heard it: *click*.

Turning around, I stared at the handle in shock. The door automatically locked upon being closed. Reaching to my side to search for my key, I came to the sobering realization that I was locked out of my apartment wearing a robe with no pockets. At any moment, a pizza guy was going to be arriving at the door for the drop-off. My apartment wasn't even on street level, which meant that entering my apartment through the balcony would require me to essentially scale a wall and climb through a bush to get in through the unlocked back door.

So, there I was, living the life of Hollywood glamour, breaking into my own apartment at eleven at night, with absolutely no shame. That is, until the pizza guy pulled up while I was caught in the hedge outside my apartment. As he carried my pizza down the sidewalk and approached the lobby, I was frantically losing my battle with the residential foliage. When he heard the rustling and looked over, all I could muster was a mortified, "I'll be right there!"

Considering it's Hollywood, that probably wasn't even the weirdest thing he saw on his shift that night. Regardless, after I finally summoned the strength to get through the patio entrance, I couldn't even make eye contact with him.

Very quickly, I realized how different L.A. life was from what I was used to. Everything happened fast, and no matter how prepared I thought I was, I could have never predicted how quickly my life would change. Unsure of what filming a reality television show would entail, I went in sticking to what I knew: my readings. Being kept entirely in the dark about who I was reading or where I was going proved to be a double-edged sword. On one hand, not knowing the circumstances I'd have to perform in forced me to trust my intuition from the get-go. On the other hand, that unpredictability and being put on the spot made me face my social anxiety.

On my second day showing up to work, I was driven to a residence in Calabasas and was told only that a client was interested in a reading. It would be filmed, my producers explained, but they did not divulge what for. At the time, I had only filmed about four celebrity readings, so this was still incredibly new territory for me.

After winding our way up through a gated community, I walked up to the door of a large, Mediterranean-style estate. With every step that I took down the elegant driveway, I visualized everyone from Oprah to Stevie Nicks opening the door. This would be a scenario I'd play out in my mind with every client I'd visit on the show. After all, not knowing what I was walking into meant that anyone could be on the other side of that door.

Seconds after knocking on the door, my stomach was in

knots as I waited for the client to answer. That moment between the knock and the reveal of the client is one of the most nerve-racking parts of my job, because it could literally be anyone.

On this day, the door swung open to reveal a recognizable face, bright lipstick and all: Khloé Kardashian. I couldn't even process what was happening, as I stepped through the doorway with the camera crew behind her, catching my every word and movement. I felt like a deer in the headlights.

As we—and a camera crew—shuffled down the hallway, Khloé led me to her living room, where I saw two statuesque figures sitting on the couch: Kourtney and Kim joined in on the reading. In that moment, I realized that I wasn't being filmed for my show. I had unknowingly walked into my own appearance on *Keeping Up with the Kardashians*. Quite the introduction into my two-day-long television career!

In the moment, the experience didn't feel real, and I couldn't gauge the magnitude of what was happening. I hadn't seen many episodes of the show, but the fact that I was granted the opportunity to appear on such a successful platform was deeply humbling. I hoped that my appearance would illuminate what I do for an audience of viewers who might not be too famil-iar with the subject of mediumship. In no time, I would come to realize how quickly my appearance catapulted me into the public eye. I was asked about what transpired in nearly every interview I did, even months later.

After providing some intuitive advice and sharing some of

the impressions that I was picking up about the residence, the experience was over before I felt it had even fully started. My nerves held me back during our first meeting, so I was excited to meet Khloé and her mother, Kris, on the second season of my show, to elaborate on these impressions. In such a short period of time, I found myself making more personal growth in my self-esteem than I had in years, as I proved to myself that I could navigate even the most harrowing of social situations.

As I got into the groove of filming my show, I had no idea what would come next. Adjusting to doing readings with a camera crew was a challenge, but my primary focus was how people would respond to the readings once they aired. After all, considering that the show was to be titled *Hollywood Medium with Tyler Henry*, my readings would focus on only a sliver of my actual clientele: bona fide Hollywood celebrities. I was the furthest thing from pop-culturally aware, and didn't even have much of an interest in the industry. Though seemingly glamorous, the prospect of reading celebrities sounded more like a challenge than a perk. So far, the celebrities I'd met had been lovely, but I feared others would have big egos. I came from a town that was far removed from glitz or glamour, and the clients I knew best were real salt-of-the-earth types. How would I compare when matched with such huge personalities?

I tried to think of it in the same way I had thought of my

first, nerve-racking group reading—the pressure would only make me better and stronger. Of course, throughout my experiences reading celebrities for the show, I've learned how much diversity there is when it comes to fame, in backgrounds and temperaments. Some were laid-back, some weren't; some you really vibe with personally, and some you don't. But as ten readings turned into twenty, I was moved to see how many sincerely honest moments were shared, as the clients opened up throughout the readings. Even the more guarded personalities seemed to yearn for an authentic, human connection. For all the perks that come with being a celebrity, how a client handles the downsides of fame reveals more about their mental states than anything they could ever accomplish professionally. I realized quickly that many celebrities lived a life of being equated with their roles or credits, as though their worth was intrinsically equal to their accomplishments.

This mixture of visibility and pressure to stay relevant makes for some interesting complexes. Depending on the personality of the client, how each individual handles attention varies. Some withdrew inward, others reacted to the vulnerability of a reading with humor or deflection. Regardless of how the client initially reacted to a reading, my process was still the same.

On some level, the fact that I didn't recognize most of my clients put them at ease. While they were used to journalists interviewing them about their latest projects, they weren't used to the vulnerability that came with opening up to someone who knew nothing about the roles they were synonymous with. With every reading conducted, I became more confident in navigating the reading, regardless of who the client was. Being starstruck would be a hindrance to my process, and more than anything, that's about ego, not spirituality. I wanted to delve into the relatable elements that celebrities harbored within their seemingly unrelatable lifestyles. I wanted the show to help spread a message of self-awareness through the transformative healing that readings facilitate. If a celebrity—who has spent a lifetime establishing necessary boundaries—is able to open up and explore the most difficult parts of their human experience, then I hoped the viewers at home would find that vulnerability inspiring in their own lives.

While there are many perks to doing readings on a television show, there are definitely downsides. Spiritual communication doesn't bend to the will of television, which means that there are hurdles to overcome. These sessions can last for hours, which makes the tight schedule of production consistently unpredictable. When I do a reading, I believe I am telling the individual what they are meant to hear at that time, and I don't change myself or my process just because cameras are rolling.

In the moment, information either makes sense to the client or it doesn't. I am careful to not get into the cynical mindset of viewing information as a "hit" or a "miss," despite what the client thinks they know. In doing this work, I know that even if a client doesn't understand a piece of information in the moment, it still often has relevance that is discovered later on. Time and again, I'd see a detail about the client's family that could only be validated from other family members' input. Yet in the world of television, if a camera isn't rolling, then there's no way to document the follow-through of certain messages. For this reason, I suggested that follow-up readings be done and filmed with clients to see where the information inevitably landed. Having the clients bring family members to watch the readings behind the scenes also proved to be a great way of getting validation and sharing the reading.

In addition to having a television show, my life changed drastically after doing readings on television shows including *Dr. Phil, Today, Dr. Oz, The Talk*, and *The View*. In going on such public platforms to explain what I do, I was faced with an array of opinions. Some were believers from the start, and others required me to jump through hoops to prove myself. Regardless of the public's take, I understood that the best explanation I could ever give is a reading in action. What many viewers didn't realize was that in order to even be considered for appearing on certain shows, I had to read countless people behind the scenes to prove my legitimacy. Having a television show gave me some credibility, but people still needed the firsthand experience in order to give me the go-ahead.

Though I was able to change the minds of many skeptics, with visibility came exposure to something everyone in the public eye deals with: hate. Having observed the reactions to other famous mediums in the past, I knew what to expect. In the minds of cynics, if a medium is asking for validation, then he must be fishing for information. If a medium relays a detail without "fishing," cynics assume the medium must have discovered that information through research.

Defending myself got old—and quickly. Despite the fact that clients gave testimonials that I delivered information that was never discussed openly, cynics conveniently ignored any details they couldn't rationalize. Whether it was telling Loni Love about her grandmother's cow-shaped cookie jar, or Kris Jenner about a private discussion she had the day before getting a window replaced, details like these simply had no rational explanation.

These were the types of details I most aimed to receive in readings. Even though I was kept in the dark about who I was reading or where I was going, I knew that in reading celebrities, their lives were obviously very public. I found great satisfaction in bringing forward information that they'd never discussed in interviews or autobiographies, and this was the standard the clients expected me to meet. Doing a reading for an unknown person whose life wasn't plastered in the media meant that getting names and dates were great validating details. But with celebrities I had to deliver details that the public couldn't possibly know.

In getting exposed to a wide public in such a short period, I didn't have time to get caught up in negativity. Showing the world that life doesn't end at death was my number one priority. Getting caught up in antagonism or about how I looked was pointless and superficial. Despite being in an industry so focused on glamour and appearances, I never had the time or energy to worry about how I looked or what I wore. I dedicated my energy to navigating the intense emotional moments I faced—all while trying to cope with challenging feelings of my own.

Until after I'd filmed season one, I didn't fully process all of the emotions that came with being given a television show. I attended the so-called upfronts at the Radio City Music Hall, an entertainment industry event where celebrities and journalists come together to discuss what's coming up in the world of television. Along with the rest of the massive audience, I was herded toward the assigned seating, I took my place, with Jennifer Lopez, Khloé, and Kourtney all within surreal proximity. Alicia Keys and Miley Cyrus gave speeches, and before I knew it, midway through the event, I heard a familiar voice thundering from above me—my *own*.

In all my sweaty glory, a clip of my reading with Snooki was shown as the entire audience watched—and I nearly melted in my seat. I had no idea that clip would be shown, and it hit me in that moment just how much my life had changed. The very thing that once alienated me now included me in a group of people that were interested in, and celebrated, that difference. It felt liberating.

I view the show as an opportunity for the public to talk about, and see the universal experiences we all have, with grief. The clients, not myself, are the true emissaries for this awareness. By bravely responding and sharing, they bring these issues forward, and it's a role they aren't used to. Most are accustomed to keeping their private lives, and especially their emotional lives, very private. You can't blame them. With invasive articles and news segments dissecting the most minute celebrity details, many public figures try to keep their image as bland and media-friendly as possible. But it's *good* for their fans to see their raw, vulnerable sides, too. From the earliest days of filming, I felt privileged to help each client share a part of her story, with the hopes that it will help others. Though I didn't recognize the vast majority of the celebrities who opened their doors, most of my viewers did. Knowing that there were grieving people at home, who could turn on the television and watch a celebrity share her own relatable experience with grief, was humbling and gratifying, for sure.

I hoped that regardless of the client's background or belief, by the end of a reading they'd leave with at least a nugget of clarity in being able to better overcome difficult situations.

If clients went in with the mentality of being a "tough nut to crack," then I had to do extra work to overcome their fears, while simultaneously trying to help them. As they say, you can lead a horse to water but you can't make him drink. In the same way, a client can be read effectively only if they're willing to explore their past and the emotions that come with it. One such example happened early on in season one.

One of the first readings I ever did for the show was with Tom Arnold. His reading was one of the most challenging, yet defining, experiences of my career. On the day when I showed up to work, I had no idea I would be reading a total skeptic. As I mentioned, to increase the show's authenticity, production went to great lengths to ensure that I never knew the identity of the celebrities I was scheduled to read—as I prefer it.

I only vaguely recognized Tom at the time, from an episode of *Celebrity Ghost Stories*. Though he showcased a sharp sense of humor throughout our visit, I wasn't familiar with his professional work as a comic. As my mom drove me to the reading, I felt like my environment had changed so much. Here I was in Beverly Hills, on my way to a mystery celebrity's house, to be filmed for my own television show. That part seemed way too surreal. Yet despite these strange circumstances, some things remained the same. Whether I was headed to the dairy in Hanford or a mansion in the Hollywood Hills, my mom was always by my side.

With Tom, I would face skepticism to a degree I never had before . . . and it was going to be televised! As Tom sat across from me quietly, he held his hand over his face. I picked up on his reservations, but they didn't slow down the images that came through. It was a heavy read. As I brought through his mother, she came through with an apology for not being the mom she now understood that Tom deserved. Now that she saw what a great parent Tom had become, she was proud that he'd ended the cycle of emotional abuse.

My only focus was on the message, but I also feared that Tom's need for evidence would prevent him from accepting the sentiments his mom so clearly delivered. Boy, was I wrong. As I would later find out, Tom made the shift from skeptic to believer as I spoke. For him, the strongest evidence I could have ever brought forward were the details his mother referenced to describe their complicated relationship. Details, he acknowledged, he had never discussed openly.

It's funny—I never know how a client is going to react, or what's going to elicit a response. I might think a person would be most affected hearing the name of a loved one, but I often find that they react more to the content of the specific messages. The spirits know better than I do what will really hit home. Mentioning a grandmother's name is one thing, but having a grandmother *remind* the client of a childhood memory that they shared makes a far bigger impact.

I know one of the most helpful things about my readings is that they provide a sense of reconnection. Even if they aren't a cure for grief, I really think they aid in the grief process. Sometimes, getting the validation that the relationship with a loved one continues beyond death is all a client needs to move forward—with a little less heaviness in their lives and a little more love. I've always rationalized that if a viewer at home can get a sense of peace from watching the healing that happens on-screen, then my reading isn't just about reconnecting two people. It's really healing many people. Fundamentally, that's what my passion is all about. Whether in Hanford or Hollywood, my intention will always be the same: to show as many people as I can that love lasts forever. The bonds we forge in this world never break.

5

The Bigger Picture

As word of my readings spread, more and more people reached out with the expectation of having an experience like one they'd seen on television. Refining my ability was, and will always be, a humbling process. As much as my clients could validate information immediately, they were often surprised when I'd focus more on what didn't initially make sense. I held myself to a standard of at least 80 percent immediate validation, allowing for the balance of messages to be followed up later with other loved ones, in search of confirmation. I found that it was often the validation that came from people outside the reading that was the most poignant. For me as a medium, it presented my biggest challenge. With who, exactly, would a message find relevance? But when the message would finally land, I was often shocked at how wise were loved ones on the other side to involve others.

My job is to deliver what I feel and see as best as I can, and the rest is up to the spirit communicating and the client validating. If a spirit is unclear, or a client just doesn't get it, there isn't much I can do! Luckily, that doesn't happen very often, and I've been consistently awestruck by the bizarre or confusing messages I've received that made *perfect sense* to their recipients. Sometimes they are later explained and validated by close family. Because context helps frame information, I think of a reading like a puzzle; sometimes you have to keep trying different angles until all the pieces fit. As each individual piece of information connects to the whole, it reveals a much larger picture.

If it weren't for the client listening and being open to hearing the message, the seemingly random symbols, feelings, and impressions that come to me wouldn't be much of a gift at all. The gift of reconnection comes from the details getting validated and placed within the proper context.

In order to provide a clear, strong, and concise reading, I also have to rely on the communication skills of the departed, which are incredibly diverse. Information comes through differently every time, which keeps me on my toes. There's never a time when I'm not learning something new about myself, my ability, or a spirit's ability to deliver messages.

Individuals will communicate in the best ways they can, using my five physical senses. Though I'm primarily visual (thus clairvoyant), I'm often surprised by the messages that are delivered through my other senses, whether it's smelling a perfume, tasting someone's favorite meal, or hearing a song that has sentimental meaning. Oftentimes it's the details that I receive through these additional sensations that help "flesh out" what the individual is trying to communicate.

A spirit's communication style tends to reflect their strengths in the lifetime they lived. Often, people who were visually oriented in life tend to better communicate with symbols and imagery, which are some of the easiest signs for me to read. Though they no longer have a body, spirits who were more physically expressive in life can still send information through my physical body. Souls who have a more emotive orientation sometimes take the direct approach by communicating their messages directly into my emotions. This deeply personal form of connection is my least favorite, because it's both the most draining and the least detailed. An emotional impression can help give me insight into the sentimental aspects of a situation, but for anything more specific, I have to hope for additional impressions to help clarify what's coming through.

One of the first times I was struck by how uniquely spirits deliver impressions was in the middle of a lengthy group reading. About three-quarters of the way through, I was hit with a pain. It raced up and down my spine, finally collecting at the base of my neck. This was clearly a spirit, but as hard as I tried to focus my intention for additional details, nothing else came.

Just radiating neck pain. This was not only uncomfortable for me, but it also felt too general to share with a room of thirty people. Regardless, I decided to go ahead and say it out loud, in the hopes that acknowledging the sensation would encourage the spirit to send through more specifics (or to move on, at least). As soon as I did, I noticed a woman in the back row, who had previously looked inattentive, sit up straight. Was this my gal? My sender also became more engaged, and the awful neck pain quickly spread down to my feet, which tingled with numbness. Wincing, I sat with the feeling. Before long, the numbness turned into a more specific sensation, like my feet were covered with abrasive sand. It was quite bizarre and certainly one of the only times my *feet* had been involved in a reading!

Unsure of what it could mean, I did the only thing I could do, which was just to go with it. I described out loud the sensation of my toes immersed in grainy sand. I felt a little silly, but I noticed the woman in the back row stare back harder, with apparent recognition. Her reaction brought forward a sensation of warmth emanating from my forehead, and a sudden and surprisingly unpleasant feeling of two lips pressed against my own! It was so jolting that I nearly ran off the stage (that was a first!). It was hard to explain, but given my negative reaction, this was no romantic kiss. As I composed myself, I could only make an educated guess based on what I was working with. Whoever was connecting wasn't giving me any visual cues, a name, or anything really useful. But I had to try my best.

I went with what I felt was the most likely interpretation. As I paced the floor in front of my expectant and somewhat confused audience, I described the feeling a final time, and then asked: "Does anyone understand? Do any of you know, perhaps, someone who may have had mouth-to-mouth resuscitation?"

I specifically made eye contact with the woman who sat in the back row. For the first time in more than an hour, she stood and spoke up with a shaky voice: "That's for me." And then she explained: Her dear friend had recently broken his neck in a fatal cliff-diving accident. As he was dragged onto the beach, she had performed mouth-to-mouth in an effort to buy him potentially lifesaving time. As she spoke, I felt the distinct warmth of lips on my forehead. When I described this to her, she validated that she did indeed kiss his forehead shortly before the ambulance arrived and EMTs pronounced him dead.

Thankfully, the information landed where it was intended. I couldn't help but marvel at the specific communication style of this spirit, with every message delivered through touch. It was highly unusual. The woman explained that in life, she didn't know her friend to be particularly verbal. Yet at every gathering, he was always the first to give everyone a hug or a handshake. He taught his nephews and nieces wrestling, as his way of showing love. "Actions speak louder than words," she recalled him saying. It made sense, then, that he would not only communicate with me this way, but that he'd prioritize the *actions* his friend took in his dying moments—the mouth-to-mouth, the kiss. He was thankful for his friend's final efforts to save him and make him feel loved in his last moments in this world. These meant more to him than words.

In a reading, the communicator dictates what comes through. The analogy I use most often is that of a blank canvas. In a reading, I essentially have to be a clear vessel to receive information without bias. The most capable spirits come through and paint the picture of their lifetime, their transition, and what they want to say by using my senses as their tools. As you might expect, the same brushes yield very different results in the hands of different artists. While some souls are of the super-realism school, painting images that look like photography, others look more like a Picasso. They give me angles and fragments that aren't exactly literal, which can feel like interpreting a Jackson Pollock painting.

Chest pain isn't super-helpful in the reading process, if I don't have a vision to distinguish between a heart attack and lung cancer. The smell of perfume is hard to describe to a crowd. And so I always strive to connect with spirits who communicate more visually and who provide greater detail.

To gain insight into the spirit communicating the messages, I make a point of asking the following three questions. When some impressions last only a few seconds, this becomes especially essential:

1. How much am I resonating with the individual on the other side?

Regardless of how a spirit chooses to come through, my first priority is to ensure that I have as clear a connection as possible. If it doesn't seem like I'll be able to interpret what I'm receiving, I set my intention to "ask" for more details. If a spirit isn't equipped to communicate fluently using just one of my senses, I prefer they engage multiple senses. This gives me more clues to what they're trying to convey. Basically, if making my head hurt is a spirit's attempt at indicating a stroke, they aren't going to get very far, unless they're able to engage my other senses to help me distinguish a stroke from a skull injury.

2. Considering how capably this spirit communicates, how much is he choosing to share on this topic?

Once I've established a clear connection, it's time to allow the messages to flow. Ideally, once I've acknowledged and moved my attention to a single impression, additional images and details will fill in, usually elaborating on the previous one. Pauses in communication are normal—in fact, essential—for me to understand when the spirit is done "discussing" one subject and is moving on to the next. It's important that I notice these pauses when they happen, because if I misread a pause in communication, I'll assume the details that follow apply to the previous ones, and it will skew my interpretation of the overall read. These moments of silence act as a period in a sentence, bringing completion to one topic, so that another subject can be established.

However, there is a difference between pausing and becoming entirely silent. When a spirit has been connecting fluently and then suddenly "goes quiet" about something, I'm often left wondering why. For instance, there have been many cases in which souls who contributed to their own transitioning (what we might call suicide or assisted suicide) come through clearly for their living loved one, delivering plenty of messages—and yet they shut down all attempts to discuss their passing. This is fairly common, and I assume that in these cases, the departed soul is either still learning about why their lives ended in that way, or is not willing to remind their family of the tragedy. Instead, they choose to focus on what they value more: their lives *before* transitioning and the lessons learned therein.

Other times, those who've transitioned themselves will immediately accept accountability, give their explanation, and try to comfort their living loved ones. What those on the other side are willing to bring up is entirely dependent on them, their level of growth, and the understanding they've acquired through their individual process. Just as in this realm, we all cope with large life events differently. Second to birth, death is the largest life event we experience.

3. How does this spirit prefer to communicate?

Souls who lived as visually oriented people will usually communicate with vivid imagery (clairvoyance). Individuals who resonated in life with sound and music may convey messages to me through noises or song lyrics (clairaudience). Sometimes I'm able to figure out a spirit's life occupation, based on the way they present information. In this life and the next, we communicate using points of reference with which we're familiar and comfortable. Our consciousness continues beyond death, as does our intention. These two elements comprise spiritual communication.

Along with receiving, prioritizing, and interpreting impressions, I'm also looking for underlying nuances. By focusing not only on what's said, but also on how, I get a very specific glimpse into the personalities coming through. Readings are an intricate process that involves not only being receptive to my client, but being *especially* receptive to my client's departed.

When I was younger, the more spirits that came through, the more I asked myself, why? If everyone who comes through is at peace, why do they feel so insistently the need to come through? I have come to realize the perspective death provides, that it gives those on the other side a whole new understanding of their lives. Considering that they're still bonded to their loved ones, they often feel it's important to share these after-death epiphanies with the living.

Whether it's delivering a much-needed message, resolving a

conflict, or aiding in the healing process, our loved ones come through to us because they want to share what dying taught them about *living*. For a long time, I thought this healing was one-sided. The most obvious healing happened when the client in front of me understood a message from a loved one coming through. Over time, I came to understand that souls on the other side benefit from delivering messages to their loved ones, as well. In sharing new perspectives and understanding about the elements and dynamics that played out in their lifetimes—which they may not have realized at the time—immense healing happens for *them*, as they continue along their spiritual paths.

Ego

Departed souls are able to recall their lives. They still have perspective, and their personalities still come through, but almost all are more enlightened versions of their living selves. They have grown to understand the impact their life choices made on others. Without an ego to defend, spirits are more inclined to resolve conflicts and accept accountability. By accountability, I don't mean something rooted in judgment, persecution, or self-recrimination—those are human concepts. I mean the kind of accountability that's necessary for spiritual evolution.

When most people think of having a "big ego," they usually mean someone who is cocky, self-absorbed, or narcissistic.

These definitions represent only a small sliver of how the ego influences the human experience. We are all running around with some mix of both positive and negative self-esteem, and the amount of each usually depends on our ever-changing circumstances. Between and among the two, the *ego* is found.

Our egos are our beliefs about ourselves. It's an identity of our own creation and conditioning that doesn't reflect who we truly are as souls. Yet, as human beings, our egos are developed from infancy and maintained throughout our lives. We think of our talents, abilities, and personalities as who we are, but these are all capabilities we have, not the defining features of our soul-selves.

A massive part of our egos has to do with our conditioning. From birth, we're being conditioned to feel certain ways about our environment, ourselves, and those around us, based on what we're told. For most of us, our parents are our first teachers. They influence how we learn to define our environments, and even more deeply, ourselves. If your parents have negative and fear-based impressions of the world, so might you. Or, at least until you recondition otherwise. Think about how getting validation from a parent fills us with a sense of worth, and being reprimanded fills us with shame. These are powerful emotions that shape and form how we react, how we feel about the world, and most significant, how we feel about our roles in it.

Usually, we aren't even aware this is going on. It's incredibly difficult for living souls to see past this hardwired ego. Even

when we contemplate our egos, we contribute to our egos—
how trippy is that? Just the act of thinking about ourselves
puts a wedge of disambiguation between "I" and "other." These
thoughts shape the ego structure that we carry with us throughout our lives:

"I am not good at taking tests."

"I am smart."

"I have bad skin."

"I am better than you."

"This outfit makes me look fat."

The ego resides in the "I" and the "me" of these thoughts.
Ego might seem like a basic and unavoidable part of being
human—and it is. After all, you couldn't function in a modern
society without some semblance of ego. It's a big part of being
human, and it provides endless opportunities to learn about
ourselves and others. However, big problems can arise when our
self-images become distorted, inflated, or diminished (and they
often do).

Our egos do a masterful job at weaving together the parts
of ourselves that we think are actually us. We feed our egos by
attaching agreeable attributes to our identities. When someone
contradicts us and we feel the need to be right, it's our egos that
feel threatened and want to mount defenses and counterattacks.
With these primitive emotions captaining the wheel, we can't
possibly interpret information properly. When we feel bad for
overreacting, our egos beat us up for being short-tempered or

petty—which our egos themselves caused us to be! In our internal power struggle, we want our opinions, feelings, and behaviors validated—but why? It's because part of us lacks genuine security.

Though it might be feasible for some Buddhist monks to completely detach from the ego, I'm not holding my breath for the rest of us. Having an ego is a fundamental part of existing as a human being. The best we can strive for is identify when our egos are "coming out to play" and take the steps to correct unhealthy, unproductive conditioning.

I put such an emphasis on the ego and conditioning, because they're two parts of the human experience that define how we, as individuals, navigate through this world. Though we're not responsible for where we come from, we are responsible for where we go. We are more than just our conditioning. We are capable of growth and change.

One of the most fundamental processes that helps us gain perspective from letting go of our egos is what I call a *life review*. Upon transitioning, each and every one of us will acquire an experiential understanding of the impact our actions and inactions had on others. When I explain life reviews, I don't want to give the impression that it's a one-time screening of a movie reel of flashbacks. Rather, it's a gradual, organic interlacing of growth, perspective, and understanding of universal interconnection. We go from the perspective of an individual human to a perspective of infinite existence—and our part in it. Souls come to understand their human lives in surprisingly forthright ways. Out of fear or shame, living people often struggle to take accountability or acknowledge shortcomings. When we die, we understand that those emotions only weigh down our lives, and we are finally able to release them. These are subjects that spirits make a point of bringing up again and again in readings—souls who've been dead for forty years, who in life never did much introspection about thoughts and feelings.

During my reading with Christopher Knight, the actor from *The Brady Bunch*, he was shocked when his deceased father came through and took accountability for his poor parenting. This was due, in part, to his father's life review on the other side. As his dad communicated with me, he made it a point to say that he fully understood the impact his dysfunction had on his family, and he apologized for never seeing it in life.

Christopher's first response was, "Is there growth after death? Because my dad would have never apologized in this lifetime."

It was clear that to Christopher, his father's actions were still a sore subject. I explained that, based on the messages that were coming through, there was indeed growth after death. When the ego was lost, perspective took its place. If someone has spent an entire lifetime repressing their emotions, being stubborn for the sake of being "right," and prioritizing his pride over their relationships with family members, they no longer prioritized these things on the other side.

Death shows us the impact we made on the bigger picture, in the short time we had on earth. These epiphanies don't come from a place of judgment or punishment; they result from natural growth. It isn't punishment that leads a deceased family member to take accountability for being emotionally distant from their family. More meaningfully, they come to this understanding on their own, once their ego is taken out of the mix. On the other side, they had no pride to defend, no stubbornness to invest in.

By sharing his new, larger perspective with his son, Christopher's father was able to provide closure and healing to his living family. Through this, he found closure too.

A fetus can do nothing to stop its own process of growth and, finally, birth. The death process acts as a rebirth, and the growth, change, and perspective we acquire in transitioning are the natural results of an expanding consciousness. It happens to even the most jaded people (and a single incarnation doesn't define an entire soul). As our states of existence shift and develop, deeper understandings of our roles in the universe are birthed.

When people imagine being disconnected from their egos, many are initially uncomfortable. What would it mean to separate ourselves from everything we *think* we are, all our abilities and talents and accomplishments, all the things we've been taught make us *us*? In this lifetime, most of us are only aware of our one current incarnation. For as long as you've been on this earth, you've been referred to as a single person with a name and a unique identity. But it's important to remember that you are still *you* without your ego, identity, name, traits, or even your body.

When we transition, our veil of ego is lifted and we come to an understanding of just how interconnected we are. We don't forget our lifetimes, but our sense of self is no longer limited to a single incarnation. We go from seeing one perspective over (hopefully) eighty to ninety years, to seeing the impact this lifetime made in an entire universe throughout time and space. Souls are able to recollect and convey the personality traits they had in life—mannerisms, quirks, and defining features that help make a connection recognizable to their loved ones. However, just because someone comes through and acknowledges a trait or dynamic that identifies them, it doesn't mean they're still limited to these characteristics on the other side.

Reincarnation

Reincarnation is a subject I get asked about in almost every reading. It's one of the most intricate, mind-blowing processes into which I've occasionally gained insight. Growing up in a conservative Christian household, reincarnation was a foreign subject that was never discussed with any seriousness. Yet as I continued doing readings through the years, I realized that I was being told about reincarnation indirectly—it was just so different from any way I had ever thought to define it, it took me a little while to catch on.

It was pretty clear from the get-go that as souls, we never stop evolving. People learn in this life, and they are capable of coming through and acknowledging growth from the other side. From there, they continue their soul journeys, expanding upon their experiences and obtaining wisdom. That much I understood.

Yet nothing could have prepared me for an event that began when I received a call from a banker. He was a self-confessed cynic who had heard about me from one of his acquaintances. Since I could tell he was more contemptuous than simply skeptical, I couldn't agree more than halfheartedly to do his reading. I was taken aback by how frantic and unhappy he seemed. It was clear that I was his last option for some issue he was facing, but he wouldn't say what it was. He also made it clear that he didn't expect that coming to me would help.

The day of the appointment, he showed up with a tight-lipped expression. As I closed my eyes and concentrated, all I could feel initially was his reluctance. It was definitely frustrating, considering he had sought me out. Yet beneath the reluctance, I began to discern the true root of his emotions: fear. As his fear flowed through me, I was definitely intrigued. Why was fear such an overwhelming presence in this man's energy?

Then, the first vision: a mother. From the perspective of a child, I saw a woman from a different era being dragged away. She was screaming and begging; the child was helpless and terrified. I was certain this was a deceased loved one coming through, but the math was puzzling. The era was reminiscent of the 1930s, and the stern man before me could have only been in his mid-fifties. The child would now be in his nineties. Was this about a grandparent losing a great-grandparent? I tried to push for additional details, but nothing came. That was my guide's way of saying, "That's the message; you have all you need to deliver it."

So, I did. I looked the man in the eye and told him that I knew he was contemptuous. I wasn't sure why he was here or how I could help. I was having only one, traumatic vision that I couldn't expand upon or explain. As I shared my vision, I thought he was about to laugh at me or get up to leave. Instead, he nodded. He explained that the client who referred him to me was his wife. He said that since he was a child, he had been plagued with recurring nightmares taking place in 1930s Berlin. In each dream, he woke with a terror of losing a woman he didn't even know: his mother from another lifetime.

This nightmare had been ignorable until he met his current wife, at which point the plaguing dreams began to reemerge with new force. He shared that both he and his wife felt a connection to that period in history. In fact, they both felt they had a mother/son connection with *each other*, and they were unsure of how to tell anyone or what to do. This was certainly a first! I had no idea what to say. It was one of my first exposures to past lives and, more profoundly, the idea that past lives could interfere with current ones. All I could do was encourage him and his wife to go to therapy to deal with the unique issues they were experiencing.

For a while, I felt confused by the past-life-related subject matter that came up in readings. Whenever it would appear, it was always with clients or individuals who were dealing with unexplainable, consistent hang-ups or afflictions that couldn't be explained otherwise. Many of the clients who came with perceived "past-life" issues had already seen therapists and psychiatrists. They had tried as many outlets as they could to get relief. For them, I was a last resort. Seeing a psychic to discuss something so intangible seemed "almost silly," they'd tell me. In a sense, they were right. I didn't feel entirely comfortable discussing a subject around which I could barely wrap my mind.

So I didn't. I just said what I saw, and I never tried to offer any explanations. At the end of the readings, I'd share with clients some of the more random images that I couldn't logically fit into their present incarnations. Often, I'd get shocking feedback that an event I saw didn't happen in *this* lifetime, but that I had described a phobia or other unexplainable aversion specific to the client. This would make both of us wonder if there wasn't something more to it, maybe from a past life.

The more I thought about it, the more it made sense. After all, if we keep evolving spiritually, wouldn't it make sense that we'd require more than one perspective to learn from? If this incarnation is possible, who's to say that more than one isn't also possible? My interest in reincarnation was piqued as I began reading about the subject in depth. I searched for information that would resonate and inform this conspicuous gap in my worldview. I was especially curious as to how all this fit in with communicating with the dead. After all, if people reincarnated when they died, how was I able to communicate with spirits? Why weren't they in a new incarnation?

The answer didn't come in books. It was revealed only partially, as I became more familiar with my own process of communication. Once I discovered that some people came through and spoke on "behalf" of others—presumably because they were the stronger communicators—I realized it was possible that the souls they were speaking on behalf of might be unavailable. Was it because they had reincarnated? With help from an individual's guides, insightful messages could still be relayed about a previous incarnation to loved ones who knew that person, without that spirit necessarily doing the communicating directly. Another dynamic I came to contemplate was how soul contracts might involve entire groups of people—and in some cases, they could choose to hold off on reincarnating until everyone can come back together.

Some of my strongest communicators have shared their

experiences with reincarnation, especially when I've set my intention to learn more about it. They explained that reincarnation provides a means to continue learning lessons one might not have learned in one lifetime. Upon transitioning and exiting our physical bodies, we still hold on to full memory of that incarnation. We are still capable of recalling it when we "come through." On the other hand, most of us *don't* remember our previous lifetimes in our current incarnations. Remembering too much would hinder the lessons we're meant to learn this time around. If we were hung up on a previous lifetime, or missing our family and friends from a previous incarnation, it would be massively distracting. One life at a time is plenty to handle and learn from!

Even when individuals reincarnate back into this realm, a medium can sometimes "pick up" on the previous lifetime they lived, read information, and even deliver insights the soul learned after transitioning. A soul doesn't need to be communicating directly from the other side for me to receive information about it. It has this information ingrained within it, wherever it may happen to be.

I can't claim to know exactly how this process works, how many lives we live, who reincarnates, who doesn't, and when—nor, especially, who or what controls the process. But I've picked up on enough past lives that I'm convinced these are part of a soul's journey. The implications of what this says about our interconnectedness and the evolution of humankind throughout history are mind-boggling. It is one of the greatest mysteries of life and death, perhaps so intricate and complex that our brains are simply not capable of understanding. And that mystery, that infinite series of question marks, may be a lesson in itself.

6

Signs from the Soul

You would think that after well over a thousand readings, I would reach the point of having more answers than questions. However, my gifts have only led me to conclude that the world is far more fascinating, mysterious, and multilayered than humans can possibly imagine. I am but a humble conduit for greater forces at play.

I've been amazed to witness not only the effects of readings on clients, but also how messages from beyond can have far-reaching impacts on others. And they don't have to travel through me; spirits are also able to deliver messages by manipulating situations in people's lives. They do this through synchronicities—seemingly orchestrated or coincidental events that send a message.

Not only have I witnessed startling synchronicities in my

own life, but I have also found myself part of synchronicities in the lives of others. I don't always know in the moment that I am being placed in someone's path, but in hindsight, the indications were always there. One such event occurred on a lunch date with an acquaintance—let's call him Jim—who would end up becoming one of my closest companions. As I settled into my seat, he and I went through the usual small talk that comes with getting to know someone. As Jim spoke about his siblings and where he grew up, I would have occasional flashes that showed me insights into the subjects he glossed over.

This dilemma was popping up in many of my blossoming friendships: I usually knew more about the person than they knew about me, at least in the beginning. On one hand, it proved to be a great way to empathize with new people in a unique way. On another, it often made me feel as though I understood others more than I was ever understood.

Continuing the conversation, I started feeling the psychic pull that precedes many of my readings. I assumed I was getting a message for one of the many people dining in the cramped eatery (it happens more than you might think!). In a moment of social awkwardness, I told Jim that I was going to need to talk through what I was feeling, to establish where it was meant to be delivered. Thankfully, he was quite intrigued, and when I had permission to share and was able to relax, the details started to flow with ease.

"I'm getting a reference to Doris and a story about someone shooting himself." I paused, as the sound of a gunshot rang between my ears.

"While cleaning a gun, specifically," I continued. As I spoke, I could tell that none of what I was saying was registering with my friend, though he did continue to listen, openly and eagerly. After a few moments, he asked what we were supposed to do next. I was disappointed—it didn't seem to apply to him, but still, a conflicted feeling sat in my gut. It felt like I was meant to deliver the message *to* him, but it didn't feel like it was *for* him. It didn't make any sense—even when spirits referred to people outside the reading, they usually established the relationship to, or the name of, the intended recipient. More confusing still, I wasn't feeling the presence of anyone who had died of a gunshot wound. I was just seeing a story about an incident, with no connection to anyone present.

As the night wrapped up, I couldn't shake the feeling that I was supposed to somehow *do something* with the information that had come through earlier, even though I didn't know what. The more I analyzed my feelings, the more I felt confused. I knew that trying to draw rational conclusions based on incomplete information only leads to misinterpretation. It's always better to deliver messages exactly as they come through, if I want comprehension and validation. The spirits know what they want to say, without my own opinions confusing things or altering the message. So I chose not to interpret anything, nor to bring it up again.

Ultimately, this proved to be a good choice. The next morning, I woke to find my phone buzzing with many missed calls, all from my Jim. When I finally picked up, he was eager to tell me that he had checked around to see if the information rang any bells within the family. To his absolute shock, his cousin proceeded to tell him the story of *his* grandmother, unknown to Jim, whose name was Doris.

Just before Doris died, my Jim's cousin had been on the phone with her, and they'd been discussing *another* family member's recent shooting accident. Doris explained that all she knew was that their family member had survived. Doris hung up the phone with her grandson, promising she'd call him back later with the full story.

That call would never come. Shortly after Doris got off the phone, she passed away suddenly, while sitting in her rocking chair. She never got the chance to tell her grandson the full story. So the two details that came through in the restaurant—the name Doris and the gun accident—were confirmed. This was one of the strangest pieces of validation I had ever received. Jim's cousin's grandmother had never even known Jim, but because Jim did knew her grandson, she was able to seize the opportunity to come through. Though I was happy the information connected, I was absolutely confused by how that connection was even possible. There were so many degrees of separation, seemingly.

That's the thing: seemingly! With time and experience, I

noticed more and more how interconnected are those on the other side. Being in our realm is a bit like being on a street level in New York City. If there's a car accident two streets over, you won't be able to witness it from a ground-view perspective. However, if a window washer happens to be on the building thirty floors above me, then he will be able to see the accident as it happens.

The window washer is just as human as I am. It's simply that from where he's standing, he can see farther down the street. In the same way, spirits on the other side are souls just like us; it's just that where they're situated allows them to have a broader perspective. With that idea in mind, it made sense that Doris would have been able to see what was happening in her grandson's life, and with whom he was associating. Beyond that, she was able to see into the life of her grandson's cousin, and so find me, through whom she could communicate.

As my guides explained to me, those on the other side have many incentives to reach out and communicate with the living. The following are the most common reasons *why* loved ones want to send signs and messages to their loved ones, and how it affects everyone involved:

1. The departed want us to know that life continues on, so that we on earth can live freer lives, with less fear.
When we die, we understand fear and its role for human beings in physical existence. Fear is the physiological, instinctual moti-

vator that tells us to avoid perceived danger, in order to keep our bodies alive. It spills over into our psychology, as well, and we experience fear of loss, fear of pain, fear of the future. Upon death, this driving force ceases to exist. Fear, and the purposes it serves during our human experience, no longer apply to a soul. That's tremendously freeing!

Like ego, fear is not inherently bad. In moderation, it's a great tool for protecting our bodies—for instance, in the event that we're being chased by a bear. But it can also hold us back, or cloud our vision. After death, when we're no longer minding a physical body, we can finally appreciate the beautiful opportunities that adversity, conflict, and challenges gave us in life, and how we learned by overcoming them. Once our egos are gone, we're able to look more objectively at situations that made us afraid in life. We can see the true lessons we were meant to learn in our previous incarnation—lessons our souls never forget.

Fear keeps our energy, intention, and focus in this realm. Time and again, souls come through and acknowledge that letting go of their fear was the key to transitioning smoothly.

2. The departed have an enlightened perspective to share, which can improve the quality of life of those they left behind. Not only do spirits desire to show us that life continues on, but they also want to help guide us. So much can be learned from those who've transitioned from the human experience, and take it from me, they have a lot to say about it! Whether they want their loved ones to learn from their mistakes, or they want to take accountability for certain actions in their lifetimes, these spirits can deeply aid the healing process for those on earth. They can also provide support, encouragement, and advice to improve our quality of life. They have gained perspective and want to benefit us by sharing it.

One profound example happened with a client of mine, a shy girl around my age whose father had passed away only months earlier. She came to see me, because a month after her father's passing, she began having vivid dreams of him nightly. In these dreams, her father appeared exactly as she remembered him, only with a stern aura she rarely saw from him in life. As he stood in front of her with crystal clarity, he told her that she needed to leave her boyfriend, because he was being unfaithful. The first night, she rationalized that the dream was a result of her subconscious insecurities in her relationship and the fact that her father was weighing heavily on her mind. On the second night of the same dream, she began wondering if it wasn't somehow a combination of a visitation and subconscious projection. By the third night, she was concerned. The last thing she wanted to do was share her experience with her boyfriend, whom she was happily in love with. Talk about awkward! After a week of being haunted by the same unnerving dream, she turned to me for advice.

Was it just a senseless dream or an actual visitation? I wasn't getting much of an answer from her father's spirit—no matter how hard I tried to connect, I couldn't feel his presence. This was super-confusing. If her deceased father was so urgently trying to communicate a message in dreams, you'd think he'd show up when given the opportunity to employ a medium.

It turns out that his connection to his daughter was so close and private, he wasn't going to elaborate to a total stranger like me the serious and personal details of the situation. This, she confirmed, was exactly how her dad was in life: if you weren't family, he didn't open up to you. Though I would have assumed death would have given him some perspective on interconnection, it was clear that he was still in the process of shedding his ego. Growth isn't instant, after all.

My client described her dreams in the same way I'd heard countless visitations depicted: super-vivid. Many report that the dreams felt almost like real-life memories. Whereas normal dreams are often nonsensical, inconsistent in chronology, and varyingly vague, spiritual dreams have an unmistakable sharpness. They also tend to be remembered as short interactions, regardless of time elapsed. To an intuitive person, dream visitations are conspicuous and very difficult to ignore.

Six months later, my client reported back that she and her boyfriend had broken up. Though at no point did she tell her boyfriend about her deceased father's message, she did test her suspicions by going through his phone as he slept. Sadly, her father's advice proved true: her boyfriend had been sending inappropriate texts to another woman for nearly three months. Although not every spirit that comes through is as relentless as this client's dad, our loved ones do try to offer insights and indicate opportunities in our lives.

3. The departed fulfill their own soul lessons by communicating, having their voices heard, and being able to give back to those they love.

One would assume that the person getting the reading has the emotional release, but the same can be said for the spirit delivering the message. Oftentimes, souls are chomping at the bit to communicate an insight they had after passing. In some instances—in which spirits come through persistently, with urgency and repetition—I've concluded they needed to deliver a message in order to move forward in their transitions. In these cases, the spirits coming through aren't unhappy, they're just on a mission. It's like if you've ever felt the urgent need to resolve a conflict with someone you love, or share with them something life-altering. I've detected palpable joy and relief when such messages are delivered.

4. The departed want us to know that we aren't alone.

The spirits of those we love want to remind us that their energy is always with us. We are interconnected, throughout space and time. Pain and sadness are temporary, but their love for us is eternal.

I've had clients who were lonely, depressed, and clearly struggling. While I can't say that connecting with their loved ones healed them completely, it did seem to provide real comfort. As a species, we are hardwired for connection. We are our best selves when we are sharing and communicating with others. Our interconnectedness is made even more apparent on the other side, so the spirits emphasize again and again that we are all meant to help one another. We are never truly alone—with every interaction, we are connecting and making a difference in the lives of others.

5. The departed want to reassure us about their deaths, and about death in general.

This ties in to the first point, but many spirits want to communicate their experiences of the dying process—which are overwhelmingly positive. Time and again, they describe an overwhelming tranquility and release from fear shortly before crossing over. Some say they felt an all-inviting presence appearing as a light. Others describe it as feeling the presence of God. Still others say they felt an immense relief of physical, emotional, and mental pain. All are natural parts of the dying process, which predicate "rebirth" on the other side.

Birth is actually a perfect metaphor: you can think of the waves of tranquility, resolution, and nudging to "move along" a bit like the contractions that transition a baby from one world to the next. These "soul contractions" are not painful but pleasant, and they help move hesitant or fearful souls from a binding state of low vibration, to a higher state of transition. And just as a fetus in the womb doesn't understand all of the change and growth he or she will experience after being born, departing souls can't fully conceptualize the next world they're about to enter.

Just as some physical births are more straightforward than others, the same is true of transitions into the next life. We all go through a process of releasing our human fears, and some of the ugly feelings that come from them, such as resentment or greed. For most of us, this natural process helps us detach from worldly matters that would hinder the lessons we're meant to learn in the next state of existence.

However, there are always exceptions to the rule. Though it is rare, some people resist transitioning immediately after physically dying, making their process less conventional. Though we all transition to the next realm, how we get there can be just as unique as we are, depending on our individual processes, where we're coming from, and what we need to learn.

I know that in general, if an individual is able to release his fear-based attachments to this realm, it generally allows for a smoother transition. However, some individuals, for diverse reasons, may be less willing to let go. In these cases, the transitions may be more of a process; they might even need assistance from other spirits. Such assistance almost always comes in the form of guides—individuals who go through more laborious transitions never do it alone.

To simplify massively, here's an analogy:

Imagine that you and two other people, all unrelated, are planning to visit California. You live only a few hours away, have a car full of gas, and can reach your destination with ease. One of the other two, however, is located in France and must go get a plane ticket, fly for many hours, and finally arrive in California after a more laborious and time-consuming process. The last person is located on the opposite side of the earth from California and has only a rowboat at his disposal. All three of you are going to the same place, but how you get there and what you experience along the way are completely different, depending on circumstances and the resources at hand.

Going through a longer or more intricate transition isn't punishment—it simply reflects that a soul needs to fully understand where it's coming from, before it continues into the next state of existence. The soul in the rowboat has the means and the resources to reach his destination, but his process looks a little different, and he may need some help from guides along the way. Just as we all have varying degrees of self-awareness in life, everyone's individual passing is tied to his capability and willingness to let go of earthly attachments and ego.

When people come through, they never seem to reference a hell or even facing judgment on the other side. Instead, they are forthright about their actions on earth, acknowledging the tolls their actions took on the lives of others. As we transition, we all go through a process of understanding the ripple effects our actions have on our surroundings. We're able to look panoramically at lessons we taught others and that others taught us, more objectively than we ever could in life. With ego gone and empathy and perspective amplified, the life review process allows for a multidimensional learning opportunity. Not only can a soul reflect back on her lifetime from the earliest moments, but she can also reflect on her part in a *much* bigger picture.

This process is both humbling and healing. Individuals who come through often acknowledge that by seeing how their lives made a difference, they were also able to appreciate those that made a difference for them. Oftentimes, this means that they acquire a deep empathy for people who have hurt or wronged them. They see clearly now what a wrongdoer's intentions were, his rationalizations, and all of the conditioning that put him in that place. They are able to find, and fully embrace, radical forgiveness.

When we understand that our roles in the universe surpass any single lifetime, we begin seeing how interconnected we truly are. That means accepting the true depth not only of our own soul's existence but also that of everyone around us. Inevitably, we learn these lessons in the transitioning process. However, if we can come to understand these concepts in life, our view of others can deepen and grow. We can learn not to take things personally, to understand that behaviors are the results of conditioning, and to make conscious efforts to understand others instead of automatically reacting to them. As a result, our lives will change drastically for the better.

Doing readings on a daily basis reminds me constantly how connected we are to the living and the dead. The insight we gain upon death—how our actions affect others—is something we can and should strive to understand while we're still here. The saying "We judge others by their actions, and ourselves by our intentions" comes to mind. We don't have to wait for a life review to judge others by their intentions, and perhaps even ourselves by our actions.

One of the first instances in which I saw all of these dynamics come together involved a client who had recently lost her mother. Their relationship in life had been rocky, to say the least: battling the crippling effects of bipolar disorder, my client's mother had been unfit to take care of herself, let alone a child. To make matters worse, my client's father left shortly after her birth, abandoning her to a woman who would devastate her childhood with abuse and neglect. After a string of toxic relationships, periods of homelessness, and a debilitating drug addiction, my client's mother finally died of an overdose, alone, as her teenage daughter slept in the next room.

The client who sat in front of me was clearly emotional before I'd even said a word. As I explained my process, she seemed so immersed in her emotions that she was only halfheartedly attentive. Wiping her eyes with tissues, I could sense how badly she wanted to explain *why* she was coming to see me. The pain in her face was visceral, but I was a little taken aback when she mentioned that she had never taken mediumship or spiritualism very seriously.

Kind of surprising, I thought, for someone who was already crying before I'd even started the reading. I wondered in that moment what must have happened for her to suddenly open her mind to someone like me. I asked her if she brought any objects for me to hold on to, to strengthen my connection, and she said she had no possessions at all belonging to her departed loved one. I reassured her that they aren't always necessary, closed my eyes, and scribbled on my notepad, as usual.

What followed was deeply unusual. Initially, I thought that two people were coming through. One energy gave me a heaviness in my gut, with flashes of dark, murky colors. These were my symbols for trauma, and they unraveled to reveal the story of a woman who spent her life in a constant flux of up and down, with a tragic ending. Psychologically trapped in an almost child-like mental state throughout her incarnation, I got the sense of a tortured person who never truly had a fair chance at life. This woman, I knew, was my client's mother.

As I took note of what I was feeling in my notebook, I paused to acknowledge the other individual coming through. Attempting to bring this person forward, I was met with a striking contrast. This woman came through more clearly than the other, with much-appreciated ease. Showing me one image after another, this new energy painted the picture of a stable maternal figure, who had tons of guidance for her daughter, whom she loved dearly. While the early visions were murky and depressing, these new images couldn't have been clearer—a sign of a strong communicator.

Immediately, I made the mistake of assuming that my client must have two mother figures in spirit, possibly one being biological and the other a stepmother (I wasn't getting a grandmotherly feeling whatsoever). But when I asked the woman whether she had two mother figures, she insisted she didn't. After her mother died, she lived with her uncle.

Confused, I revisited the information I'd written on the page and tried to make sense of it, with little success. Considering I'd received a strong connection from the second energy, my first inclination was to get clarification from her. As I attempted to look into her passing, it was clear that she had passed away close to middle age. All I could intuit was that the heaviness in my lungs indicated respiratory failure, a cause of passing I often relate in younger people to drug overdoses. This didn't make much sense, given that the energy that came through wanted to talk about my client's career, health, and well-being, much more than the circumstances that led to her transition (usually when a person passes in such an abrupt and traumatic way, that's the first acknowledgment they make to their loved ones, to provide explanation and reassurance).

Yet this woman's form of reassurance was different. She clearly communicated the name of my client's boyfriend, acknowledged a specific surgery that was coming up, and even reminded my client of a specific conversation she'd had only the day before our reading. Any shred of skepticism the client had entered with dissipated as she validated all of the details I was sharing with her, all related to her personal life. The only problem arose when I went on to describe the woman who gave me that information. I assume you know, by now, where I am going with this.

As I described her mother's personality as stable, communicatory, and self-aware, the woman who sat in front of me looked down and shook her head. It didn't take a psychic to see that she was still confused. And at this stage, so was I.

In a state of panic, I closed my eyes and tried to see anything more from the woman who communicated so clearly, and so maternally, but was deeply confusing to me. In a brief flash, she impressed upon my mind three numbers in succession: 555. I was deeply thankful for the series of numbers, as it felt important, with the familiar tug of urgency. I wasn't at all sure what it meant, but I did what I always do: simply trust what's coming through.

As the words left my lips, my client had one of the most emotional reactions I've ever seen in a reading, to this day. I didn't understand such a reaction to a random series of numbers. To me, they meant nothing. But to her, 5:55 a.m. was the time displayed on the digital clock that sat by her mother's bed, the night of her death, at the moment she walked into the room and discovered her body. They were three numbers she'd never forget.

After her mother's death, she had gone years without any noticeable signs or feelings that her mother was still with her, seemingly disproving any faith she'd once had in life after death. Yet, for unexplainable reasons, she had recently begun seeing those three numbers, 555, everywhere. She explained that at first, it was only occasionally noticeable—she'd see the numbers and experience a painful, but brief, memory of walking into her mother's bedroom and the horror of what she found there. But with each passing day, she noticed the series of numbers more and more. Whether she was at the post office or the grocery store, she saw the number on everything from price tags to addresses to receipts.

One evening, she came home from work and was shocked to find her alarm clock frozen at that exact time: 5:55. Considering it was actually around 9:00 p.m., she could no longer deny that her mother might be trying to send her a message. Not knowing whether she was having a mental breakdown due to unresolved trauma or her mother could indeed be reaching out, she decided to pay me a visit the very next morning.

Given this information, I had no doubt that I was indeed communicating with my client's mother. Having had her identity validated, I now simply had to reinterpret everything that had come before it. Unsure of what to do, and with nothing else coming through, I took a simple approach. I ripped the paper from my notebook and placed it on the desk for her to see each impression I'd written, for both of the contrasting energies.

As she eagerly squinted to read my earlier description of the first, muddled mother figure, I watched as tears continued to pour from her eyes. With her finger sliding down the page where I had written, "Bipolar. Neglectful. Poor communicator."

"That's the mom I knew in this lifetime," she said in a quiet voice.

Chills filled my body as I processed one of the most profound informational downloads of my entire life, all coming from the mother who so eagerly wanted to connect with her daughter. As a pressure welled at the crown of my head, I was inundated with flashes and sensations, small expressions that helped describe a much larger dynamic.

In that moment, I understood what I was meant to say. I could feel her mother's strong presence guiding me, clearing up the confusion I was having in the interpretation process. As explanations flooded in, I first became aware that synchronicity was indeed how my client's mother attempted to communicate. She had tried in earlier instances, but my client was so caught up in her grief that she wasn't able to pay mind to the signs that were there.

The next realization provided a sort of bizarre epiphany. Both energies I was feeling were literally the same person. My client's mother had achieved so much growth on the other side since passing that she was like a different person in every way. She had evolved so much as a soul that I made the mistake of thinking she was an entirely different person. Nowadays, I know that when I receive impressions from an energy that doesn't communicate, I'm simply reading information off the querent. That information is about the spirit's life on earth, which can contrast *greatly* with the state of mind achieved on the other side.

In life, my client's mother loved her in the only way she was capable. Plagued with mental illness and chemical imbalances, the mother she knew thought and operated through a severely damaged filter. It was so warped that it corrupted the loving person she would have been, had she not been afflicted.

Now her mother wanted to give her daughter the guidance she wished she could have given her in life and to be the parent she deserved—only now, from the other side. Most important, she wanted to share that she was always with her daughter, that she loved her and watched over her, and had used the synchronicity of the numbers that represented her transition to grab her attention. If she sent the reminder often enough, she hoped, her daughter would notice the signs and eventually find a way to communicate.

Our loved ones don't get mad at us when we don't notice the signs they send, since their primary intention is to share their love for us. These signs are a testament to that love, but they can be missed for a variety of reasons. Sometimes it takes the more obvious signs, like the one that prompted my client to visit me, to feel a strong connection. It's important to remember that even if they're not noticed, it doesn't mean they're not there!

While everyone who comes through seems to acknowledge growth and perspective, some individuals are nearer the beginning of their journey, and therefore have varying degrees of understanding. We all seem to get there by different routes and speeds.

Perhaps surprisingly, this doesn't seem to affect whether spirits can communicate and connect. Early on as a medium, I struggled to connect with souls who had died recently. As time has gone on, however, I've found that even the recently passed can come through, since everyone learns how to navigate that realm on their own terms. Personally, I still prefer not to do readings within the first six months of a loved one's transitioning. This has nothing to do with the spirit, and everything to do with the client—it's essential that the grief process happens naturally. The raw emotions that come with recent loss aren't usually conducive to accepting the insights a departed loved one provides. On my end, too, it's extremely distracting. I end up picking up on the client's strong emotions, and it can overpower my focus. I have a limited amount of headspace, too, and it leaves fewer faculties available for the spirit to deliver messages.

In the case of the client discussed above, her mother had

been trying to send her signs that she was around. Had she been more open to intuition, she may have noticed those signs earlier. If synchronicity is one of the most powerful ways the other side communicates, being able to recognize those synchronicities is essential. This is done through intuition. With our guides there to assist us, and our loved ones eager to connect, intuition is the neglected piece of the puzzle. If synchronicity can be likened to a loved one trying to call on the telephone, then intuition is the means to answer that call.

With the number of signs loved ones try to give, it's no surprise how many stories we've all heard about profound or unexplainable experiences. And yet there remain so many people who wish more than anything they could feel just *one* sign from a loved one. Even if it hasn't happened for you yet, it's not out of reach. With enough awareness, belief, and trust in your own intuition, you can train yourself to notice the signs when they're there—and you'll discover that these messages are *abundant*.

Both the intention and the capability of our loved ones to communicate with us from the other side show how connected we are to them, even beyond death, and even if we don't realize it or feel it in a given moment. The very fact that spirits reach out from the hereafter shows us how much they love us. This is a dynamic the dead can teach us about life: that reaching out to those we love, and appreciating them—whether they're with us physically or not—can help both souls grow, evolve, and heal.

7

Clairvoyant Q&A

This chapter provides answers to my most commonly asked questions, ranging from my experiences in spirituality to how I've been informed by my guides and spiritual interactions.

One thing is obvious: the universe and the mechanisms that dictate spirituality are so complex, we can only understand a small fraction of what the other world is like. This holds true for even the most intellectually brilliant and spiritually enlightened among us. It is a realm vastly different from our own. I don't pretend to have the answers to every question. I can only catch glimpses here and there, and give my best shot at interpretation. Over time, some of those interpretations have gained more credence, which I judge based on consistency, confirmation, and repetition. Other explanations still elude me, and I've had many otherworldly experiences that baffle me to this day.

For many of the deeper, more spiritually oriented questions I'm asked, I will often resort to analogies and metaphors to help break them down. Some of the subjects have complex answers, and this is the best way I know to help explain them. I'm the first to admit that many of these answers are incomplete, as the world beyond our own is mysterious and boundless. But where I can, I provide examples from my life and work that support the conclusions at which I've arrived. You'll draw your own conclusions, based on what resonates with you.

I know that it's my duty as a medium not only to pass along messages to my individual clients but also to communicate what I know to the world at large. I don't know why else I would have been granted these abilities, if not to share them! And so, I will continue to write down, document, and share my beliefs as they evolve or are validated through personal experience.

Do the spirits of animals come through?

Yes, absolutely! Over the years, the energies of pets have come through with surprising consistency. I've brought through many souls that have lived as animals, from dogs to cats to birds. It's clear that the connections all living beings make with us and each other continue on, the same way their life forces do. I don't "talk" to animals per se, as I'm not a pet psychic or animal whisperer. However, as I'm able to establish how humans passed and details about their lives, I'm often able to do the same with pets. I read information from their life energy, and as we've covered, that energy doesn't have to communicate information with spoken language.

I don't think anyone who has owned an animal would be surprised by these facts. After all, the companionship some animals communicate can be closer than many human relationships. It makes sense that the same dynamics would continue on. Just as one physical incarnation doesn't define our entire soul's capability, the same applies to our furry friends. For them, each incarnation has a purpose, and they're still able to communicate their appreciation and love.

One of the most profound animal connections I've experienced happened during my reading on my show of actress Jennifer Esposito. The meeting took place at a quiet bakery in New York, where I was met by an open, kind woman who presented me with a single object: a worn, well-loved bow tie.

As I held on to the bow tie and scribbled away, it was clear that Jennifer was looking to connect to someone specific. In addition to the grandmother popping in, and distant relatives trying to connect, I couldn't keep my attention away from an insistent energy that repeatedly acknowledged his name: Frank.

As I tuned in to Frank, I saw my symbol for a progressive decline—a hospital bed, which represents physical illness and deterioration. Initially, I was confused. This consciousness

clearly indicated others being involved in his passing. Yet I
didn't get the feeling of a homicide, or even someone having
to take the loved one off life support. This, I could tell, was
different.

It wasn't until I saw a vision of golden fur that I realized
I wasn't bringing through a deceased family member at all—
well, at least not in the *traditional* sense. The image of a golden
retriever flashed through my mind, as I held the adult-size bow
tie in my hand.

With each word I said, Jennifer seemed more and more
floored, and she provided me with immediate validation.
Frankie, she explained, was her golden retriever who recently
had to be assisted in his transition. She stood up, clearly moved
and with tears in her eyes. She went into the other room to get
a photograph to show me. It was of her beloved dog, Frankie,
wearing the very same bow tie I held in my hand.

Though I didn't get an articulate message from the dog's
soul, I could feel his appreciation for not having to endure a
prolonged suffering. With each validation I received, I could feel
his love for Jennifer grow. Frankie was overjoyed that his owner
was acknowledging him. It was clear that Jennifer had immense
feelings for her dog, and she credited him for helping her get
through the ups and downs of life. But to the dog, Jennifer was
his *whole* life. The fact that he was capable of coming through so
strongly was a testament to the incredible love that bound them
together, even beyond death.

Do animals reincarnate?

I believe that just as we continue on, the same principles apply to all beings that are capable of consciousness. Reincarnation is a mind-boggling subject, but at its core is the idea of the evolution of the soul. All states of consciousness offer learning opportunities, and as long as those experiences are retained at the soul level, there's purpose in proceeding on to subsequent incarnations.

One example comes from a private client of mine, whose home I visited to do a reading. His German shepherd had passed away in the home three years prior to the reading, and their bond had been inseparable. After the dog's passing, his remains were cremated and placed in an urn, which sat prominently on the top shelf of my client's bookcase. After a long grieving process, my client decided to rescue a puppy from a shelter, to help ease his pain and loneliness.

Shortly after arriving home, the puppy immediately ran to the exact spot in the house where the German shepherd had passed away. As the days turned into weeks, it was obvious that this was the new dog's favorite resting spot. It was an odd spot at that—a cramped corner of the laundry room. Over time, the puppy got used to his new home. One day, my client was surprised to come home after work to the sound of excited barking, coming from in front of the bookcase. Initially, he was unsure what was holding the dog's attention for hours on end. When he realized that it was potentially the urn, he decided to move it out of the house, to see if the barking would ease up. Strangely, it didn't. My client was left seriously confused.

As the months passed, my client began noticing an increasing number of signs that he couldn't explain. The new dog seemed to have a lot of weird hang-ups that pertained to the dog that had passed. The skeptic in my client wondered if the puppy wasn't simply detecting the scent of his former dog and responding to it. Yet when his new puppy began consistently waiting to be fed in the area where his former dog's food bowl had sat, he began wondering if there wasn't something more to it. He even noticed that when he walked the energetic puppy, it would naturally follow the old, shorter route the old German shepherd preferred in the last years of his life. The only way my client could rationalize these bizarre incidents was to consider that his previous dog had reincarnated into this new pup. By the end of our session, he found great comfort in the idea that his new puppy could be an incarnation of his former companion. Truthfully, I wasn't sure what to make of it—but at the very least, I felt that the behavior of his new pet showed that there was a connection between the two pets who shared love and companionship with their mutual owner.

Do you believe in God?
Yes, but first I have to explain my definition of what I call God. You might have noticed that whenever I discuss spirituality, I

tend to avoid words like *heaven* or *angels*, instead preferring to say "the other side." If I talk about angels, it's under the broader term "guides." This is more than just a matter of semantics. I avoid words that come with preconceived associations, particularly if aspects of those words do not resonate with me entirely. For the sake of being as concise and accurate as possible, I avoid labels that could imply a complete agreement with fixed beliefs.

The word *God* is a loaded one, there's no doubt about it. But the higher power I believe in is a spiritual God, not a strictly religious one. In order to fully explain my thoughts on the matter, it's important to share my religious background, so you can understand the context. I grew up in a practicing Protestant Christian household. I attended both youth group and church services as a child and teenager. I always found religion fascinating, so much so that in my earlier years, I considered becoming a minister as a career path. It seemed that for a lot of people I knew, their interpretation of the faith was entirely dependent on what a preacher told them. That always seemed limited to me. I truly wanted to understand the history and context of the doctrine I aimed to live my life by. And so I researched Christianity to the best of my ability, with every resource I had.

Fundamentally, I knew there were some deep truths being shared within the church, especially when it came to the feelings religion instilled in me. These were undeniable: when I'd stand in church during a sermon that spoke to what was happening in my life, I felt a spiritual kinship with the entire congregation. I felt a connection to a higher power that seemed to answer my prayers in the form of spiritual guidance. It was a feeling that I just didn't get outside church. When we came together through prayer, song, and worship, it was like we were channeling something far bigger than any of us could imagine.

Yet, as fulfilling as church could be, it was only comforting and interconnecting when I felt safe. I quickly realized that just as church could inspire, uplift, and inform, it could also alienate and destroy a young, impressionable person's sense of self-esteem. This was especially true if the congregation or the preacher had rigid ideas about how people should be. In coming to understand the historical context of the more dogmatic parts of the Bible, it became clear to me that the Bible should be taken for what it is: a book written by humans two thousand years ago. They lived in different times, in a different culture, with laws and ethics that are no longer entirely relevant to modern society. Many Christian churches still take these stories and mandates literally—even the outdated sections that vilify women and gays, and normalize slavery and polygamy.

Another aspect of church that I grew concerned about was how commonly fear was used to scare churchgoers into good behavior. And what was the number one source of that fear? The Christian idea of hell. That one perplexed me entirely. By age thirteen, I'd already read and interpreted at least a hundred messages from the other side. I had yet to meet anyone who came through and communicated that they were burning in hell. It just didn't match up with what I was hearing every Sunday.

More than that, the thought of hell was plainly contradictory to the idea of a loving God. If God is all-knowing, all-powerful, and ever-present, then why would such an awesome and wondrous force waste His time demanding to be worshipped, by pain of eternal torture? It sounded like the kind of behavior one might expect from a base and tyrannical human being, not an all-powerful, all-knowing Creator.

I always tried my best to be objective in my journey through faith. In the end, I found myself caught in a mental battle between having faith in organized religion, versus trusting in my own personal spirituality. The two are related, but there is a crucial difference. It is undeniable that the hope, connection, perspective, and moral compass that religion provides are powerful tools for spiritual growth. But religion requires faith above all; it is a testament of unconditional devotion to a specific doctrine and style of worship. It also requires study, effort, and maintenance. My spirituality, which as you can imagine is very strong, comes from within. It requires no maintenance beyond that which flows naturally from living life. I have only to trust in a few fundamental truths, which have always resonated with me more than any doctrine written or preached by men.

I made my shift from the belief in a *religious* God to a *spiritual* God. I definitely believe in an inherent creative force that's responsible for—and interconnects—all that is. Although I was raised to believe in an anthropomorphic God who passes judgment and metes out damnation or heavenly reward, ultimately my pursuit of God led me inward. I now view God as a force that we are all not just the result of—we are also a part. What gave me that unexplainable feeling of fulfillment as we worshipped together in church was not the "rightness" of the words we were singing together or the doctrine we were supporting. It was the feeling of connection between people in a congregation, as they expressed collective gratitude to the Creator. This feeling of fulfillment doesn't require religion at all. It is available to any group of souls communing through interconnected passion and selfless dedication to a force greater than themselves. My spiritual sense tells me this is where God lives. No matter how it is manifested, I know that this source connection runs through us all, infinitely.

Do you believe in possession?

Whenever people ask about possession, I imagine that they have scenes from *The Exorcist* flashing through their minds. I'm usually right about that; it seems everyone wants to know specifically about *demonic* possession. It's the idea that one could go from being in control of himself to being literally possessed by—and under the control of—an unknown, malignant force. I always hate to burst their bubbles, but I have yet to see a single case of what I would classify as demonic possession.

Most cases of supposed demonic possession in this day and age can be explained by epilepsy, schizophrenia, or other medical conditions. Obviously, when "possessions" were more common, hundreds or thousands of years ago, there was no modern understanding of the brain or of mental illness. People came up with narratives that gave them comfort and a sense of control over something they feared. Undiagnosed schizophrenia was deemed the work of an anthropomorphic demon. It was given a name and a backstory, so it could be "driven out" by a shaman, and in later years, a priest. Exorcisms were the made-up "cure" for maladies no one understood.

Though I'm skeptical of so-called demonic possession, I do obviously believe that entities on the other side are able to influence our lives. Whether that comes in the form of synchronicity or through us intuitively picking up on signs of their existence, I've noticed that many living people can experience a perceptual shift due to spiritual forces.

Is this possession? By my definition, certainly not. Getting intuitive impressions from a loved one, or noticing reoccurring signs that aid us along our paths, is another thing entirely. Though these visitations alter our consciousness, we are still ultimately in control of our bodies and minds. There's none of the powerlessness that comes to mind when one thinks of possession.

If actual demonic possession were to exist, I can only imagine it would have to present in an individual who is a deeply abled medium. Even then, I would think only under extraordinary circumstances. It might be possible for a powerful but uninstructed medium to mistake the often strong physical, mental, and emotional impressions being sent from spirits as being signs of their own "possession." But that person would have to be so receptive to information, and so suggestible, that the information he received replaced his own thoughts and feelings. Even the most gifted mediums acknowledge that as overstimulating as the gift can be, it's never so much that we lose our self-awareness or identity. For this reason, I think it's wise to first suspect mental illness, before even considering that "possessed" behavior might be rooted in the realm of spirituality.

The belief in (and fear of) demonic possession in certain religious communities only further traumatizes people who are in need of professional mental help, not spiritual intervention. I also believe that the very idea of demons and demonic possession—like the idea of hell—is rooted in fear and control, not spirituality. Saving congregants from "demons" is yet another way that organized religion can make individuals feel dependent on it. And in the process of "exorcising" the individual (from a malady they don't actually have), the victim is often blamed. The person who needs professional psychiatric care gets told that their lifestyle choices or individual failings opened the doorway for some crippling affliction that is, medically, not their fault. When it comes to spirituality, it's important that we be honest, not needlessly afraid. I can tell you that I've never seen any evidence supporting that demonic possession is real or is anything we need to worry about.

What is the most common message or theme you receive from the other side?

Though each interaction with the other side is unique, I'm always intrigued by how often they have similar themes. Regardless of each individual's lifestyle, background, and cause of passing, most souls come through emphasizing, to varying degrees, the importance of the following subjects.

1. Forgiveness. Deciding to forgive is the single most liberating choice a soul can make. Even (and especially) those who were extremely stubborn in life come through and acknowledge that whatever it was that they used to be angry about now seems silly and pointless. They frequently describe how after they transitioned, they learned to let go of the unhappiness that came with focusing on the upsetting situations they faced during their lifetime.

In the same way that a well-adjusted adult might no longer resent a childhood conflict, or even someone who bullied them, individuals on the other side grow and evolve in their understanding of themselves and others. Death is the next stage, and our spiritual adolescence during life evolves to adult maturity, upon our passing.

People on the other side often communicate that once the lesson has been learned, there isn't any point to holding on to conflict. Because our existence continues on after death, it would be a tremendous burden to hold on to one issue or another for all eternity. When a perspective is broadened enough, anger and resentment simply can't survive the process.

2. Victim versus student. Once the ego is taken out of consciousness, we start seeing how many times in life we hindered our own learning process. Feelings of victimization, defeat, and apathy aren't conducive to growth, and yet on earth, people often find themselves in ruts they find difficult to escape. Not so on the other side.

When souls come through, they often acknowledge awakening to the important roles others played in their lives. They describe it as similar to realizing you are actually an actor in a production, both playing a part and watching others play individual characters. Even when the main characters clash in a scene, the actors still can like each other off-camera and be the closest of friends. In a similar sense, those who caused us conflict in life were merely fulfilling roles—on the other side, their souls and ours may be in harmony.

People also come through saying they now understand more about their self-saboteur—the part of themselves that was self-destructive and impeded their own happiness. We all have it to some extent, but hopefully we make conscious choices to overcome our own worst habits (and propensities for dysfunction) throughout our lives.

On countless occasions, people who have come through tell me that putting their pride aside would have made their life substantially easier and less painful.

One of the most fascinating parts of the transitioning process is the life review, because it allows us to see how our conditioning affected others and ourselves. When describing their life reviews, many souls acknowledge that they could have learned so much more had they applied more self-awareness and not allowed their conditioning to dictate their quality of life. For this reason, we can feel encouraged to seek more self-awareness and apply it wherever possible to our thoughts, choices, and circumstances. Challenging ourselves to find and retain lessons from the obstacles we face can help us go from a mentality of victimhood to one of progress.

3. Gratitude. For me, one of the most appealing perks of the afterlife is the heightened sense of thanks. Souls describe this feeling again and again, and I assume that this new gratitude comes along with their expanded perception. Souls say they appreciate the meanings and correlations between events and people that they didn't perceive during their physical lifetimes. Even the most jaded of people in life express immense gratitude from the other side. With ego stripped out of the way, it's much easier for souls to understand the role that challenges had in their learning process, without getting caught up in the negative emotions we experience in this realm. If the living were able to appreciate our lives as much as those on the other side, we'd be dramatically happier. We'd live every day as though it was our first and last. In fact, people on the other side often encourage us to focus on living in the present moment. It allows us to feel gratitude more fully, without hang-ups over the past, or fear about the future, clouding our minds.

Reminding yourself of *what you do have* takes up headspace that might otherwise be focusing on *what you don't have*. We can never have too much gratitude—it's grounding, and it gives us clarity over what really matters in the present (and every) moment.

Are past-life regressions valid? Are they harmful or helpful?
I believe that past-life regressions can be helpful, but I'm hesitant to encourage it. I believe that there's a legitimate reason most of us don't remember our previous lifetimes—doing so would take us out of the lessons we're meant to learn in *this* lifetime. The distractions that come with reliving past-life memories and trauma aren't usually worth our time or energy.

There are a few exceptions. For example, if someone organically has a recollection of a particularly traumatic past-life memory, they may benefit from better understanding the context of the experience. Only then will it cease to haunt them. Otherwise, if someone isn't consciously bothered by a past-life memory, then I feel that kicking up dirt from other lifetimes should be approached with caution.

Past-life regression, as we know it in the modern day, has been supported and pushed by the New Age movement. It has been packaged as a type of expansion and reconnection with a spectrum of soul experiences. I'm plenty content with what my current soul experiences have to teach me. While alive, we should do everything we can to find acceptance over the circumstances we face and take steps to better ourselves. This is more than enough to have on our plates. Going backward could have unexpected consequences for an individual who isn't prepared to cope with what they're reliving—you never know what you might stumble across accidentally!

Are tarot cards legitimate in providing spiritual insights?
Tarot cards are a spiritual tool like any other. Whether an individual is using astrology, runes, tarot cards, mirror gazing, tea leaf reading, or any other form of divination, all are tools that intuitive people can use to glean information. The tarot cards themselves hold about as much spiritual power as a deck of playing cards—which is all they were, originally. It's all about the person reading the card—a tool's effectiveness depends entirely on the craftsman's skill in using it.

Having used tarot cards myself, I believe they help a reader get into the organizational mindset that allows for information to be sorted out and decoded. The number one struggle even the most skilled intuitives face is the difficulty distinguishing precise details, especially when impressions are jumbled. Tarot cards act as a reference book of relevant symbols, giving a skilled reader a clearer idea about where each intuitive impression applies, based on their assessment of the cards.

Really, this is my belief on all spiritual practices. Each is only as relevant and reliable as the practitioner is skilled. Those who are truly *great* at divination tend to be in touch with their spiritual side and a state of mindfulness as a lifestyle. Whether someone gets herself in a receptive mindset using cards, mirrors, or rune stones, it's more about the mindset than the objects. These tools help organize intuitive information, but they don't produce it. The best diviners understand that being guided by their intuition—not just what shows up on a card—is the essence of the process.

Have you ever met any other young mediums?
I have! Young working mediums are a rarity, because it often takes people gifted with the ability years to recognize it, come to terms with it, and refine it through deliberate practice. If it weren't for the older mediums who came before us, this subject wouldn't be as widely discussed, and it would be much harder for us to come forward openly.

Meeting others in my age range, who can relate to certain experiences, is incredibly helpful. Everyone works so differently that when it comes to comparing technicalities, common ground can be minimal. Despite this fact, there's *definitely* a comfort that comes with being able to relate to others who navigate their lives with a sixth sense. Being a young adult comes with its own challenges, universally, so to have a psychic lens over these life experiences adds an incredible new layer of complication.

This isn't something that's widely talked about, because it's a bit of a taboo subject. Many young mediums struggle with anxiety, as a result of their overtuned senses and the pain that comes with feeling dismissed or alienated. Even among the older medium community, there are a lot of gifted people who struggle to cope with the responsibilities and burdens that come with having this ability. Being expected to have all the answers, or to be a cure for people's grief, can be a massive load that isn't for everyone. It's important that the next generation of mediums band together to support each other—after all, we're all in this together.

Is being a medium heritable?

I'm still on the fence with this one. I do not feel that my own abilities were inherited from either parent. Other than having a general intuition, neither of them has exhibited signs of being a medium.

At the heart of this question is whether paranormal gifts are rooted in nature or nurture. Is there a biological predisposition to a heightened intuition, or are people who grow up in certain environments (perhaps around other mediums) more likely to embrace their intuitive capabilities? I believe that though nature and nurture may contribute to how a person processes their ability, the source actually has nothing to do with genetics *or* environment.

If it's neither heritable nor situational, then I know it begs the question, why me? I grew up in a household that didn't even discuss ghosts, let alone embrace intuition or a second sight. I know that from a very early age, my extra perception was ever present, just as natural and automatic as my other senses. My only explanation is that some mediums may have a soul-purpose for this path, in certain lifetimes.

But this doesn't change my opinion that *everyone* has intuition and is capable of receiving intuitive impressions and messages—to varying degrees.

So what made my degree as extreme as it is? Well, much like we're all capable of painting, some people naturally excel at it, while others require much more practice and motivation to improve their skills. It's a nonscientific answer, I know, but it explains most of my experiences with other mediums, so far.

Can people on the other side block other spirits trying to come through?
They can, and it happens. My goal in a reading is to be able to connect with whoever is the clearest and strongest communicator of the bunch. In most cases, the stronger communicators will inadvertently "talk over" those who aren't able to communicate

as efficiently. This isn't done with any ill intention, as much as it's just the result of the process. Depending on where someone is in the ego-stripping process of the other side, they can come through with varying degrees of conviction. In one case, I recall doing a reading for a young man whose parents died due to drug use. His mother's soul came through and actually overpowered his father's energy, because his mother felt he wasn't ready to communicate the types of information her son needed to hear. In other words, my client's father was still processing his life and the meaning of his death, and he needed to focus on himself before anyone else—or so his mother determined.

As you can imagine, in group settings, I often find myself overwhelmed with overpowering communicators. To make it a little easier, before doing a group reading I set the intention for anyone coming through to do so in an organized way. Sometimes that means having everyone who passed away of a certain cause come through together, so that I can keep track of who's who!

In some cases, no matter how hard I try, I have to rely on help from my spirit guides. When they come through, they are often able to act as "gatekeepers." They allow everyone a chance to come through, one at a time. This can be massively helpful when I don't know where to start!

Do you ever receive conflicting information?
Rarely, but it happens. It's important to remember that just because someone has died, it doesn't mean they have all the

answers. Death doesn't suddenly make us omniscient, which is why souls endeavor multiple incarnations to continue learning and growing. As a result, spirits come through with a wide array of thoughts, based on their experiences. To what extent someone has come to terms with their ego tells me to what extent I should weight their opinions. If a grandmother comes through and gives the impression of not liking a client's boyfriend, and she shared that sentiment in life without a valid reason, then I know grandma's still in the process of working toward a less biased perspective. Life reviews aren't instantaneous, and just as we learn from our experiences in this realm, souls on the other side are processing what their lives meant.

I've never received conflicting information from my guides. Their egos are no longer part of their present states, and they are not biased by human concerns. These guides are able to relay details and facts without emotional investment, which is greatly helpful in understanding how things work.

Do you believe in aliens?
I do! I think that there are many forms of consciousness in this universe, and humans aren't necessarily the only "intelligent" life. Considering how massive the universe is, it's both naive and egocentric to say that we as humans must be all there is. I've never once had an alien's soul come through in a reading, but then again, why would it? If souls come through to reconnect

with loved ones, then that takes extraterrestrial aliens out of the equation (unless I'm reading Elliott from *E.T.*).

I remember Snooki asked me this question the first time we met. It was clear the idea that aliens could exist was deeply concerning—as it is to many. It's important to remember that in the same way movies and television have skewed how people view spirits in the afterlife, the same is obviously true for how we think of otherworldly beings. Because people simply don't know or understand this phenomenon, their fears get the best of them. They fill in the blanks of what they don't understand with anxieties and assumptions.

I believe that in the same way that the consciousness of another species continues on and evolves spiritually, the same applies to a species of which we're not yet aware. It's very possible that they have a completely different process or interpretation of life and what comes next, but their energy continues on, regardless. My guides have definitely come through and acknowledged that entities that we, as humans, have yet to understand, do exist. They don't refer to them as demons, angels, or anything we have yet conceptualized. I'm particularly fascinated with cryptozoology, and wonder if certain phenomena like the legend of the Mothman aren't just examples of extradimensional beings that somehow interact with our own plane. If guides and spirits are able to get in touch with this realm, then who's to say it's off-limits to other beings?

It's important not to limit our idea of aliens to little green men who abduct midwesterners in their sleep. Someday, humanity probably will discover intelligent extraterrestrial life, and I think it will be vastly different from anything people are afraid of today.

When you see a photo of someone you've brought through, do you recognize them?

Often, the answer is no. This fact tends to surprise everyone who asks the question, but I have a reasonable explanation! Most people assume my ability is something like a mix of *The Sixth Sense* and a game of psychic charades. The reality is that for a spirit to deliver information, even to a medium, it requires an extraordinary amount of effort. Souls that communicate while I'm in a waking state tend to not waste focus projecting an elaborate image of their former appearance. In dreams, it's much easier to project specific and thorough scenes, because my conscious mind isn't in the way of the impressions. In a sub-conscious state, it's much easier to receive vivid detail. When I hold on to an object and scribble, I'm able to tap into my sub-conscious side partially, to bring forward sensory impressions and fragments that get pieced together. So unless they've come through in a dream, I'm usually not presented with a specific idea of how they "look."

Instead, spirits communicate in the way humans understand best: through signs, symbols, and real-life comparisons. When a

paternal grandfather is coming through for someone I'm reading, my first clue is generally a vision of my own paternal grandfather. Most of the souls, with the assistance of my guides who
know my life and history, draw comparisons to certain situations I've seen in my life, helping paint the picture of their lives
in the process.

There is one very neat aspect to this: as I have more experiences with spirits drawing from this mental dictionary of symbols, my vocabulary grows. I can only assume that over time,
this process will continue to refine the details of the messages
I receive. In fact, my precision has only increased as time has
gone on, because the images, symbols, and parallels the souls use
have taken on more variety. It may not be as straightforward as
seeing full-bodied apparitions walking around, but I've learned
to understand this symbolic language. I think of the process of
psychic interpretation as a puzzle waiting to be solved. I get the
same satisfaction from solving it as a student might have when
settling upon the exact right word in a foreign language.

**Spirits talk to you, but to what extent can you talk to them and
ask questions?**
My ability to ask questions depends entirely on the clarity of the
connection. Paranormal communication is direct. It's the tele-
pathic linking of one consciousness to another. It's only possible
through the projection of intention—something both I and the

consciousness on the other side are doing. The receptivity of either side can vary, but setting the intention to project (that is, concentrating upon) a specific impression is the fundamental means to communicate a message.

Sometimes the message is a question. When a spirit comes through and requests that I ask the querent herself a question, I often find myself slightly surprised and unnerved. It's a reminder that even though spirits have a broadened perspective, they aren't omniscient. When I find that someone coming through is a particularly strong communicator, I'll often try to ask questions to see if I can receive answers. But again, the sweep of their explanations is limited to comparisons drawn from my relatively short lifetime of experiences.

At the end of the reading, I'll usually ask the client if she has any questions for the spirit coming through. Even if I don't get immediate responses to the questions, the projection of intention can stir up additional messages that can prove to be illuminating.

I find my best personal insights come from my spirit guides. Their answers usually come in the form of "downloads"—a term I use to describe intricate bundles of information on certain subjects. These streams of impressions are the basis for many of the beliefs I discuss throughout this book.

While my ability to communicate with a spirit can be dependent on his ability to communicate with *me*, my spirit guides are different. Connecting with them (when they're present) feels

like familiar territory. They're the most consistent, reliable communicators with whom I come into contact. But even so, I still
don't know much about them or who all of "them" are. With
every question I ask, I hope to come closer to these answers.

**Can you explain the symbolism that comes through in read-
ings, and give examples?**
Symbolic messages are some of the easiest, most efficient forms
of communication. Not only are they concise, but they also
often represent complicated subjects that are easier to understand when represented by a single image. Below is an example
of some of my most common symbols, and how I would interpret them.

When I'm initially connecting, I often establish the gender
of the person, even before their relation with the client. Blue
means male, pink means female. From there, if I have a vision of
my paternal grandfather, then that means that my client's paternal grandfather is coming through. If I have a flash of Tim, for
example, then I'd know that I'm bringing through someone who
died early. Spirits draw comparisons to people I know and can
relate to, with the help of my guides. If a spirit comes through
and I have a vision of my living next-door neighbor Carol, then I
know that the spirit is trying to have me acknowledge the name
Carol as being applicable to the message.

Establishing the identity of who is coming through is one

task, but delivering what they have to say can be much more challenging. Below is an example of specific symbols, and what they mean to me individually:

Bottle, red nose: Alcoholism

Cages: Feelings of entrapment, stagnation, being stuck

Circles: Cycles of behavior

Closed eyes: Being unaware of a situation

Cracked earth: Breakups, separations

Dirty window: Lack of mental clarity or perception

Double-sided arrow (<—>): Geographic distance between two people

Doves: Freedom from mental illness

Finger pointing down: Focused on oneself

Finger pointing upward: Focused on someone else

Hospital bed: Progressive decline

Lace/Veils: Marriage/weddings

Murky colors: Trauma

Ribbon: Cancer

Straight line: Closure, stability, peace

Torn lace: Divorce

White roses: Forgiveness and closure

Window: Perspective, mental clarity

On their own, one may think that these symbols would be relatively easy to interpret, assuming one understands their meanings. What becomes difficult is when two symbols come together at once, meaning that the ideas inform one another. Here's an example:

White roses (forgiveness, closure), **bottle** (alcoholism), **straight line** (closure, stability)

If I saw these three symbols presented in succession, I would assume that there was a situation around alcoholism, and that having closure with this is being emphasized heavily from the spirit coming through. When delivering this to a client, the challenge becomes figuring out *who* dealt with the alcoholism, *why* the spirit is bringing up closure with it, and *how* to convey that as accurately as possible. I may wait for an indication of a dirty window (which usually indicates that the person coming through is acknowledging a lack of mental clarity in life). If I see a dirty window, then that individual is likely trying to convey that they dealt with mental dysfunction in life as a result of alcoholism.

I can only go by what I see and feel, and I have to make educated guesses based on what's being communicated. I find that if I describe the symbols and what they mean to me, the client can usually understand where the message fits. If I just give my interpretation without any explanation of the symbols that led me to that conclusion, then I'm more likely to misinterpret. Sometimes when I describe exactly what I'm seeing and feeling the client understands the message loud and clear without any need for interpretation.

This is why it's important to rely on my other senses to receive information. If I can't make much sense out of a series of symbols, then I can usually rely on my other senses to help fill in the blanks. In a way, it's a bit like getting sentence fragments and having to come to conclusions based on what they could mean in relation to each other. By analyzing the individual impressions, I have to translate them into a coherent message.

When we don't have a physical body to communicate, we come up with methods of communication in our own way, through intention. In the same way that someone who is deaf may use sign language to communicate, symbolic gestures and sensory impressions can convey messages just as profoundly as literally speaking them.

Do all of us have spirit guides, and if so, how many?
I have yet to meet a single person who didn't have spirit guides. These extradimensional beings are capable of interacting with us on a very profound level. Our spirit guides aren't here to save our lives, or even keep us from harm. They intervene on their terms, for reasons we don't always understand. They help guide us on our soul's evolutionary paths, and perhaps sometimes remind us that we aren't navigating alone. When guides do interact with us, whether through visitation or synchronic-

ity, they are reassuring us of our paths, even if we're still in the dark.

Is it important to call our guides by name?

In the beginning, I felt like I needed to know all of my guides and all of their names. Psychics on television would often refer to their guides as their "team," and I was jealous of their closeness. I, too, wanted to know the identity of my spiritual teammates. While Sylvia Browne claimed to be in consistent communication with her spiritual guide, Francine, I have never experienced that kind of consistency. I started off with Walter being my primary guide, but then something shifted in the way my guides would manifest. In some instances, my guides would appear in a dream as a crowd of people. In other instances, it would be as symbols in fleeting visions. It was always different and varied widely. Sometimes, in dream-time visitations, they would come manifested as animals. In rarer cases, they'd be inanimate objects that represented something or communicated a message.

I've never been able to pin down all of their exact identities—if they even have them. Perhaps that's intentional, because pinning names on spiritual guides humanizes them, and there's no point in doing so other than giving us peace of mind. Names might make the idea of spirit guides more comforting, like guardian angels with names and identities. But I can accept not entirely knowing the forces that guide us through our journey of life. It is one of the most beautiful and profound mysteries, which I hope to understand more as time goes on. I also realized that if I put half as much energy into meditating and intuiting as I once did trying to figure out the number of guides I have and their names, I'd benefit much more from the direction they have to offer.

I will say, in one of the few times I was able to gain insight as to why their identities are so ambiguous, the answer was surprising. The vision I received likened their elusiveness to an actor needing to be private to play a convincing role. If the public knew too much about the actor's personal life, they might be distracted by what they know, rather than getting immersed in the character. In a similar sense, they stressed that we not focus on them and who they are, but shift our focus to the guidance they're trying to provide. Their souls don't seem to emphasize identity in their realm, as much as they prioritize direct action, and as a result—growth. Therefore, we should focus all effort toward connecting with their insights for bettering our lives. And from that, our understanding of them will evolve.

Do you have any readings that stand out from others that you've done?
Obviously, every reading leaves a lasting impression, but some affect me personally more than others. One of my earliest readings was also one of the most emotional for me, and it sticks with

me to this day. Initially, it started off no different from most. A middle-aged woman and her two teenage children came for a reading. As we sat in the small room where I did readings out of the shop, she presented a single object: a ring. As I explained my process and told them what to expect, I could feel their eagerness to connect.

The second my fingers wrapped around the ring, I saw a bottle, cages, and a clear window. That trifecta of symbolism indicated alcoholism, feeling trapped or stuck in life, and then a reference to obtaining clarity. As I described what was coming through, the woman began weeping as her two kids comforted her.

The man who proceeded to come through was insistently less interested in communicating about himself, and instead was putting the focus on his wife, who sat in front of me. Though he referenced his struggles, he emphasized wanting his wife to not feel guilt for his death. In most of the cases in which those symbols came through, they painted a pretty straightforward picture: a husband with alcoholism passed away after feeling stuck, and obtained clarity on the other side. Right?

Well, sort of. It ends up that the symbols actually meant more to the client than any interpretation I could make from them. She explained that her husband's drinking problem prompted her to admit him into a rehabilitation facility to save his life, family, and marriage. While he was getting treatment in the facility his wife brought him to, he died while detoxing from alcohol.

The symbolism of mental clarity referred to the fact that he was mentally clear before he died—with coming off daily alcohol use that spanned years, he was in his moment of death the most clear-minded he'd been in a long time. He was mentally clear enough to know something was seriously wrong, and that if a medical emergency happened while he was in rehab, his wife would hold on to the guilt for bringing him there.

As she sat in front of me, I couldn't even begin to process how she must have felt. She brought her husband to the very place where he'd pass away, with the intention of getting him the treatment he needed to regain control of his life. Her husband came through and wanted her to let go of the guilt, that it wasn't her fault, and that ultimately he knew she was just doing what was best for everyone. It goes to show that situations are often so complicated and multilayered, even I as a medium sometimes just have to present what comes through, exactly as it arrives. Ultimately, the family left the reading with the knowledge that the man they loved the most knew that they had his best interest in mind. Despite the tragic, inadvertent result of taking him to rehab, his love for his family transcended all circumstances related to his death.

Has your ability ever shown you anything revealing about your parents?
It has! Being an only child, I was always heavily involved in my parents' lives. As a result, I often saw details about their histories that they never told me. In one case, I remember being at a family get-together and interacting with my half uncles on

my mom's side. As my mom and her siblings met up after a long time of not seeing each other, I couldn't help but feel that someone was *missing*. As a kid, this was the toughest part of my gift—being overwhelmed by emotions and feelings that made absolutely no rational sense.

As the family reunion continued, I couldn't ignore a word that flashed through my mind: *Gemini*. After taking note in readings that certain symbols would be communicated with a consistent meaning, I came to identify Gemini as being my symbol for twins. Yet, without a doubt, there were definitely no twin family members in sight.

When I explained to my mom what I was feeling later that night, her face turned serious. She explained that when she was born, her fraternal twin passed away in the womb. It was a sore subject in the family and never discussed.

I'm not entirely sure why the reference to her twin came to me, but I can only assume that it was because it was a family reunion. It may have been his soul's way of expressing that he was still connected to the family he never met. Despite not getting to live a life with the family he was born into, my mother's twin still may have valued the family he watched over—and wanted them to know that he was part of the reunion, too.

Why do you sweat so much in readings?
When the show first aired, this was one of the most frequently asked questions. Anyone who has seen the show probably notices

that by the end of a reading, I'm often drenched in sweat from head to toe. This is almost always the result of people coming through too intensely. When I'm communicating with a spirit for the first time, they're not always capable of understanding the extent of what they're able to project onto me. As a result, I may pick up on serious physical pain that corresponds with how someone passed. It can be great for validation, because it's so clearly received, but it's *not* great for my body. As much as I'd prefer to only get visual symbols of heart attacks, there are times when chest pain is the only way a spirit can communicate that cause of death.

As times goes on, I hope that I'll be able to navigate readings more mentally, and less physically. Ultimately, I have very little control over what comes through, and how it's received, but I can control the delivery of the information. Once I communicate what's causing me pain, it usually dissipates, to my relief.

In some cases, my sweating is the result of something far from paranormal: set lights! The amount of lighting required to film is super-intense, and it can get really hot after an hour of being under glaring lights. But I know that if I'm sweating long before I walk into the room, it's probably rooted in an intuitive feeling, and has nothing to do with lighting.

Do children have stronger intuition than adults?
Oftentimes, yes. Children aren't biased by rationality and doctrine. They're much more receptive to intuitive experiences,

because they're much less likely to disregard them. Unfortunately, as kids get older, they are frequently told, "It's just your imagination," or, "It's all in your head," and their receptivity begins to diminish. Once certain religious beliefs (or skepticism) are introduced into the mix, we can develop a very narrow perspective that isn't conducive to embracing intuition.

I think a lot of us have had spiritual experiences in childhood that we now chalk up to overactive imaginations. But are we so sure? For instance, when I was about six years old, long before I knew I was a medium, I had a spiritual experience—but I dismissed it for many, many years. In preparation for an upcoming family reunion, I was staying at my grandmother's house, along with some extended family. My cousin and I were the only two young people staying there. We were so excited that we had trouble getting to sleep, and we lay awake in pitch darkness at 2 a.m. As I sat cross-legged on the mattress with my back against the wall, I noticed a faint light emanating from the door, which was slightly ajar. It was the light from the kitchen, I said, to reassure my cousin—but really to reassure myself! As I was offering my explanation, I was stunned by what I saw next.

Coming from the kitchen down the hall, I'm quite sure I saw a shadowy figure that stood about eight feet tall, pacing the hallway toward the door. It stood there just long enough to darken the sliver of light from the kitchen. My first assumption was that it was simply one of my tall uncles, in silhouette. When I called out, the figure glided wordlessly down the hall.

My cousin said he saw it, too, and we were determined to get to the bottom of this. I lost the game of rock, paper, scissors that would decide which one of us was going to venture from the safety of the room. I walked into the living room, expecting to find a relative playing a prank on us for not being asleep. Instead, I was met by a chorus of snoring. Every member of my family who was spending the night was fast asleep in the living room, on couches and reclining chairs. Chills shot down my spine. Whoever the visitor at the door was, he had continued his journey down the hallway—a dead end with no exits. And now I had to walk back down *that very same hallway* to return to the room! As I faced the darkness of the hall, I could feel every hair on my body standing up straight. So I did what every kid does in this situation—run! Sprinting into the dark room and immediately flipping on the lights, I proceeded to freak out and explain that our nighttime visitor may not have been a family member at all.

I know I personally had countless unexplainable experiences as a child, and I've heard the same from many, many others. It makes complete sense that children would be more inclined to have spiritual experiences. Without the years of conditioning that make typical adults jaded, children are clearer vessels, naturally receptive in their openness. I find that we as adults can be more open, too, by emulating the attitude of a child—complete, nonjudgmental immersion wherever our minds take us, with no worries about time or limitations. In other words, meditation!

How do you discern between a visitation and a dream?

People often wonder if dreaming about a deceased loved one means that it's a visitation. It's definitely possible to dream of a loved one after their passing without it being a visitation. Oftentimes in the process of grieving, people will dream of their loved ones as a means of processing and coping with their feelings of loss.

Visitations are often entirely different. They're dreams that are so vivid, clear, crisp, and unmistakable that the difference is obvious. Sometimes dreams can be both a mix of visitations and subconscious babble. For example, one may actually connect with a loved one in a dream, but the setting of the dream is entirely the product of the subconscious mind.

When spirits first started visiting me in dreams, their primary priority was ensuring that when I woke up, I'd remember *their* visitation. Given the number of visitations I would receive nightly, their intention was set on me being able to relay their message. Funny enough, they had unique ways of ensuring these dreams were *incredibly* memorable. In one case, I recall a grandfather coming through and pointing at his chest, and then I saw a massive explosion that filled my vision with orange and red flames. Startled, I caught my breath and asked the empty room, "What was *that* supposed to mean?"

Immediately the same figure came through and gave me the impression of a heart attack. Apparently, just conversationally explaining that he died of a heart attack wasn't memorable enough. I realized that he had taken extra steps to ensure he'd be unique among the countless spirits coming through in a night. He certainly achieved his goal! Later on, this same man came through in a client reading. She acknowledged that her grandfather was an over-the-top personality in life, and she was not surprised by his theatricality when coming through.

Can you share more about your experience with soul contracts?
This idea of soul contracts became popularized by the New Age movement, though definitions vary as to what exactly they are. One common definition is that a soul contract ties one soul to another across eternity. Over a thousand readings, I have encountered a lot of evidence that these connections do exist, and some souls are particularly connected to each other, over multiple lifetimes.

However, the exact mechanisms at play are likely far more complicated than the definitions that I've seen thrown around at psychic fairs and spirituality meet-ups. People are enthralled by the idea of knowing someone before we consciously *remember* knowing them. It's another proof of our interconnection, so it does make some sense. I do think that reports of unexplainable familiarity serve a profound purpose, in teaching our souls very specific lessons. I also believe that our souls are capable of entering incarnations together with cooperative intent. Though the human beings involved may not be consciously aware of this so-called soul contract, they may find that their intuition and internal compasses guide them to each other with an undeniable pull.

Soul contracts within human incarnations aren't just between people with whom we get along. Often our greatest teachers are those who challenge us and put our capabilities to the test. I've heard about amazing life lessons between parent and child, friends, enemies, siblings, and in pretty much any other relationship you can think of. Through intuition, such individuals may begin noticing indications of a soul contract—which tend to manifest as a remarkable familiarity and chemistry (which in some cases can be explosive).

The dynamics of such a powerful relationship, especially a negative or difficult relationship, can be resolved if the individuals develop a deeper understanding of the purpose each serves in the other's life. However, if no effort is made to understand the other person's underlying motivations, these negative dynamics run the risk of repeating until they're recognized and resolved. This is what often leads to toxic relationships, love-hate relationships, and codependent relationships. If you find yourself in one of these difficult associations, it's important to acknowledge the deeper dynamics at play. A lot can be learned from the buttons someone else pushes. You must remember that even if you have a soul contract, the soul contract doesn't have *you*.

I believe I saw a clear example of a soul contract between a couple who came for a reading, Jason and Tae. Both in their late teens, the two had an inseparable bond that was clearly more than puppy love. Their relationship wasn't even just romantic, as much as it was a connection unlike either had ever felt with another person. They fulfilled many roles for one another, giving the support of a parent, the love of a romantic partner, and the understanding of a sibling. Yet when times were rough, in a single relationship they had a whole family's worth of dysfunction. Dramatic peaks and valleys defined their interactions. As Jason struggled with debilitating depression, he became incapable of eating or getting out of bed, let alone maintaining his relationship with Tae. Through the course of the two years that they saw me, Tae began realizing more and more that her relationship with Jason existed to teach her about something much more than loving someone else. It taught her about herself. Through watching Jason's descent into depression, Tae was able to better understand the parts of herself that also battled with depression. These were parts that she could keep hidden around her friends and family, who were the type of people to always put on a happy face, regardless of the circumstances. By having no control over his feelings, Jason taught her what it meant to be true to her own. In learning this incredibly difficult lesson, Tae got in touch with emotions she had never explored before: she, too, struggled with depression.

Through coming out the other side of what most would consider an incredibly toxic situation, she was able to take steps to better her mental health—and, ultimately, her life.

Once Tae got help for her own depression, her relationship with Jason changed. It never lost the chemistry they both undeniably felt, but they realized that they had gotten from the other exactly what they were meant to receive. Jason got assistance with his struggle, and Tae got clarity in hers—ultimately serving as a catalyst that changed her life for the better.

Both continue to be close friends, and thankfully they no longer struggle with depression to the extent that they did when they met with me. After they better understood the underlying dynamics of their relationship, they were able to move forward in healthy ways, with an acceptance that their connection would always be there. Despite this fact, both knew that being in a romantic relationship together was no longer a healthy choice for either of them, and they chose to maintain a friendship instead. They chose a graceful and healthy way to learn from their soul connection.

What's your take on soul mates?

Okay, I admit it: this is one of my least favorite subjects. It's not that I'm unable to provide insights into clients' love lives, but I'm all too aware of the typical expectation: "Tell me my soul mate's name!"

Everyone seems to be under the impression that a soul mate is an individual that exists out there in the world, waiting to cross paths with you—your perfect match. This idea that we all have a spiritual Prince or Princess Charming out there, entirely compatible with ourselves, is not only ludicrous, but actually quite damaging. It's the kind of thinking that can cause people to sabotage their real relationships—perfectly healthy, challenging, spiritually edifying relationships—just because they face some very normal difficulty. They imagine that their "soul mate" wouldn't struggle with the same incompatibilities and differences that come with a "mundane" relationship. But incompatibilities, differences, disagreements, forgiveness, and reunions—these are the *whole point* of being human!

First of all, we definitely don't have just one soul mate. There are countless souls who exist and have existed that we could resonate with on a deep level. You could call these people "soul mates," but they aren't inherently romantic! If anything, I've seen more platonic soul mate dynamics take place, like those between parents and children. A soul mate is simply another consciousness that we agree to join in this realm.

Being in a happy, healthy, fulfilling relationship doesn't require a soul mate. It's more important that we be mentally, physically, and spiritually compatible with our partners, and that we learn from them what we can: deep lessons about love, mercy, fidelity, strength, selflessness, and sacrifice. Holding someone to the impossible standard of "soul mate," on the other hand, can lead to unrealistic expectations. Who would really want a relationship where neither partner would grow spiritually? This life has challenges for a reason! Finding the commonalities you and your partner share and balancing between compromise and acceptance of your differences is the healthiest way to evolve.

How do we get in touch with our guides via intuition?

As I've mentioned earlier, guides continue to be an elusive subject for me in many ways. Regardless, I do believe that there are ways we can consciously encourage their communication. It is the same process required to develop one's intuition: meditation and quieting the mental noise. The less distracted we are, the more room we have to receive impressions and guidance.

Communications from our guides can initially seem subtle or simplistic. Sometimes it's nothing more than a random thought that enters our headspace. You're probably used to assuming that you alone are the sole source of all your thoughts. In reality, perceiving the basic intentions of what guides are trying to communicate, and processing them as conscious thoughts, is surprisingly common. If you've ever gone to bed at night upset about a situation and then woke up with more clarity, or even the answer, it's possible that your guides were responsible for the epiphanies. How can you know? The key lies in learning the unique "language" they use to interact with our realm. Everyone has different experiences, and that's why it's important to focus less on the identity or number of your guides, and to devote energy into noticing synchronicities as they happen.

Consciously asking for a sign is a great start, so long as you are open to whatever answer you may receive.

If there's one thing communicating with my spirit guides has taught me, it's that they never act predictably. They seem to follow a greater agenda and help to facilitate our lessons in life—but in ways that far exceed our human understanding, since they have a clear insight into the interconnection of all things. Believe me, their ability to communicate through happenstance, coincidence, and our interwoven network of consciousness is just as mind-boggling as they are.

What happens to people with mental illness when they die?
I've had countless people come through whose lives involved suffering from mental illnesses. Everyone who comes through acknowledges that they are not limited by that mental condition on the other side. The same can be said for people who go through physical illness; those who pass of cancer don't have it in the next realm, it was affliction of their human body. I'm often surprised by the number of people who come through acknowledging that they unknowingly struggled with mental illness during their lifetimes. It's surprisingly common.

Through the growth process on the other side, they come to understand the root causes behind the challenges they faced. Mental illness has so many manifestations, we're just now beginning to understand and treat it properly. Especially in the cases of older generations, in which mental health care was limited, individuals acknowledge that undiagnosed mental problems explained a lot of the issues they had in life. In many cases, making this realization can be healing to the individual, because they are relieved to know that their illness is not *them*. It can also be healing when this explanation is conveyed to family members who may have suffered.

Mental illness can be compared with a "filter" over consciousness, which upon transitioning is no longer part of that person's makeup. As they review their lives, countless spirits have come through and conveyed that they wish they had received or had access to professional mental help. They encourage those who live with mental problems to get help by utilizing the resources we have access to—now more than ever in human history.

How do you tell if a medium is authentic?

First, I'd encourage you to give as little information to the medium as possible. If you're going to see a spiritual practitioner, getting a referral from someone you know and trust is your best bet. Practitioners are running a practice, and just in the same way that you wouldn't call a 1-900 number for a dollar-per-minute medical consultation, the same standard should apply for intuitive practitioners. Any actively working professional in the psychic business should have client testimonials— and not just a few they handpick for a website.

If someone really has an ability, then they'll inevitably attract a following and build a thriving clientele. Given the number of people in this world who are seeking guidance, those who are truly able to provide it will stand out easily. For this reason, I'm weary of psychics who have worked for years with few incoming clients—unless it's entirely by choice. If a psychic is accurately making predictions and providing validating information, they're going to have no problem attracting business and staying busy.

When it comes to advice, consider the source. If a professed psychic is charging ten dollars a pop and can barely keep their doors open, they should be using their intuition to find a new profession that actually resonates with them. A credible spiritual practitioner will take the time to explain his or her process and answer any questions you may have. When it comes to responding to what they may say, limit your answers to a yes or no. It never hurts to be aware of your body language, and an authentic practitioner shouldn't be staring you up and down during the entirety of the reading. You'll be able to tell where their focus is—and if it's more on you than on what's coming through, that's a major red flag.

It's unfortunate that there are inauthentic people who claim to do this work, but you can protect yourself with some common sense. And with a legitimate medium, you can have an awesome experience—there are many out there! Don't be afraid to validate, keep in mind some of the more obscure references (they often make sense later), and if you feel that someone isn't legitimate, politely get up and walk out. You'll probably get an immediate feel for whether someone resonates with you or not. Go with *your* gut!

Is it possible for someone who lived and died hundreds of years ago to come through in a reading?
Technically it's possible, but it hasn't happened to me yet. Souls usually don't see a point in presenting their former incarnations to me as a medium, unless they have a message to deliver to a living loved one. In the cases in which people lived and died centuries ago, their immediate families and loved ones have already transitioned and reunited on the other side. As interesting as it would be for Abraham Lincoln's soul to come through, there'd be little incentive on his end to deliver much of anything.

Though I'm not walking around constantly interacting with dead historical figures, I find that places oftentimes hold on to energy. That can be particularly interesting as an intuitive person, since I'm able to read impressions from events that may have occurred recently or even long ago. It doesn't mean that anyone's necessarily coming through to chat, as much as I'm able to just intuitively get a sense of what occurred in that physical environment.

In the way that actions and reactions leave energetic impressions on their environments, the same applies when I walk on a former battlefield, or an area where a homicide occurred. To varying extents, it's possible to feel the emotions evoked by what happened, without directly communicating with the person who died there.

If I go to an empty shopping mall at night, I may feel the foot traffic that was there earlier in the day. This makes going to places like New York or even hectic parts of Los Angeles really overwhelming, because there are always new energies being introduced on top of residual ones. As an intuitive, it can feel like a cluster of incoherent information that's frustrating to navigate and discern on my own. That's why intention is such an important part of connecting, and my guides help me connect with the information in a reading that the client is meant to hear.

Do you ever deliver bad news?
It depends on what you mean by bad news. Before I ever go into a reading, I do a brief meditation and set the intention to connect with the guidance my client is meant to hear. Whatever that may be, I believe it comes through for a reason. Synchronicity has taught me that few things are ever random, and if I'm reading someone, I'm there to say something that might just impact their path in a positive way.

I set the intention before every reading to connect only to information that will be helpful to my client in some way. Otherwise, what's the point in connecting? Considering that I don't believe the future is *entirely* set in stone, I generally get a sense of a person's trajectory in a particular area. If I see any unpleasant results in the forecast, I know there's something positive to be gained by mentioning it. Whether that's stopping a medical emergency from happening, or giving someone an awareness to better cope with something that's unavoidable, each serves a purpose. I much prefer to acknowledge what can be changed (unfortunately, death and taxes are pretty much set in stone). If anything, most people are needing encouragement and validation—not warnings or cautionary tales. That's why readings are often surprisingly uplifting; they validate and encourage certain life paths while helping us navigate away from ones not for us.

Though readings can touch on some pretty heavy subjects, ranging from familial issues to addiction problems, all of these subjects are generally acknowledged with a perspective "in hindsight." There isn't judgment behind these issues, so much as they are brought up to help us understand. Sometimes those details are difficult to hear, but essential for growth.

Have you ever had a situation where an individual was widowed and remarried, perhaps more than once? How do those multiple marriages play out on the other side, when it comes to who spends eternity with whom?

People are often surprised to hear that marriage doesn't really apply on the other side. Marriage—a ritualistic and legal union between two people—is a human agreement that (hopefully) extends throughout a lifetime, but not further. The vow is "'Till death do us part," after all. But it doesn't have to be a total parting. Just because legal marriage ends at physical death, it doesn't degrade the connection between two souls. I have spirits come through all the time who acknowledge that they were married to each other in life (and still clearly like each other enough to interact on the other side!).

I'm fascinated when people come through with a whole new understanding about their relationships after they've died. Oftentimes, the perspective that comes with fear and ego being taken out of the mix allows for conclusions to be made that weren't available to them in life. This means that dysfunctional marriages are explored and learned from, and closure is brought to any emotions that contribute to stagnation or negativity.

Through many different incarnations, we will love many other incarnations. Loving many doesn't devalue the love for one, and it's important to remember that. When we're talking about a soul that's infinite and expansive, the capability to connect with love from many sources is inevitable—and that's a beautiful thing!

Has what you know about relationships on the other side affected your views on monogamy in life?

Despite knowing that our souls will continue on to love and be loved by many, I still think that monogamy serves a purpose in this world for those who feel drawn to it. I don't need to know that a marriage will last beyond life to appreciate and enjoy the person I'm with. If anything, I appreciate and honor the relationship even more for what it is, because I know that it will naturally evolve as we do. People's fear of the end of a relationship often prevents them from truly enjoying what they have while they have it. I choose to focus on being thankful for how things are, in the present moment.

It's important to not confuse the significance of a relationship with its length. What matters most is what bonds are exchanged and what lessons are learned in the time that's shared.

What's the most profound message the dead have delivered about life?

Fundamentally, each individual comes through the understanding that they are merely a droplet of water in an ocean of consciousness. This expansion of our awareness is humbling, but I'm told they feel awe at the interconnections that exists between all beings. The lesson for those of us on earth is obvious: we can all strive to find that interconnection in life, by being compassionate. There's a reason some of the happiest people are also some of the most giving. In a modern society that worships the self and contributes to narcissism and insecurity, the stripping away of the ego is both a relief and a shock to any incarnation that's used to perceiving itself in one rigid way. We disconnect from the negative conditioning that contributes to self-esteem issues, mental illness, and spiritual stagnation. We are unburdened.

If there's one overall theme I could take away, it's to appreciate life in *every moment* and respond to challenges in a way that's true to who you are, even if it's the more difficult path. With the past stirring regrets, and the future provoking anxieties, it's important that we live in the present moment. It is, after all, all there ever really is.

If we can seek to be more present, we will be inclined to be truer to who we are and what we're feeling. When we can authentically be who we truly are, and be honest with ourselves and our feelings—not making decisions out of past hurt and future fears—then we are free.

Though nothing can prepare us for the process of dying or experiencing the death of a loved one, we can take steps to appreciate those we love and remind them how we feel. It's important that those we value know in the moment how much of a difference their lives make on ours—right now. After all, no matter how present we are, the circumstances of our present are bound to change and evolve, as we do.

I strive to encourage people to live their lives in such a way that they'll never need help from someone like me. When we live each day with kindness, compassion, and communicative love, there is no business left unfinished. There are no regrets or words we should have said, but didn't. There is no need for closure or forgiveness or apology of any kind.

A life well lived is not harmed by death.

Acknowledgments

Writing this book has been an incredibly humbling process that's been made possible through the stories, guidance, and support of those with whom I've been lucky enough to cross paths.

I want to first thank agent Brandi Bowles and editor Jeremie Ruby-Strauss for their dedication, patience, and incredibly helpful input in making this book what it is today. Going into this, I knew of some fundamental points I wanted to share with the world in telling my story. As a result of their support and inquisitiveness, I was able to expand upon these fundamentals and explore subjects in a way that I never had before. For their collective and individual efforts, I am forever thankful. Also at Gallery/Simon & Schuster, thank you to Carolyn Reidy, Louise Burke, Jennifer Bergstrom, Nina Cordes, Kristen Dwyer, and Liz Psaltis.

Acknowledgments

I want to thank my manager, Ron Scott, as well as Michael Corbett and Larry Stern, for being the catalysts that brought me onto the path I'm on today. If it weren't for Ron taking a chance on a teenage medium from a small town, among a sea of local actors, none of this would have been. His selfless kindness, uplifting sense of humor, and tireless determination inspire me to never stop striving to better the lives of others. Ron bettered mine and changed my life in the process. Michael and Larry's commitment to protecting me and always putting my well-being first is something I will appreciate endlessly. Their resources, endless hard work, and generosity catapulted my life on an incredible trajectory. Words can't describe how appreciative I am for the kindness they've shown me. I hope to share the compassion I was shown in my life and work.

Of course, I want to thank my parents, because without their approval and encouragement, I wouldn't have been able to fulfill my passion from such an early age. Their courage, strength, understanding, and unconditional love make me the luckiest son ever. My mother's resilience, integrity, and endless selflessness inspire me every single day. She's proof that no matter what adversity you face, you can thrive despite it. My dad's grit, positivity, and endless strength are all traits I aspire to have in the way he does. He puts the love of his child before any doctrine he was taught, and that's the way it should be. In having an open mind, my dad showed that progress is always possible, when we put love first. I love you both so much!

Acknowledgments

It takes a special kind of person to be a companion to a medium, and I'm thankful for all of the companionship I have in my life, in all the various forms. To Derric, thank you for motivating, encouraging, and inspiring me to always do my best. Having a grounding presence among a flurry of new experiences is a gift. Matt, thank you for being with me from the beginning and loving me for who I am—not just what I am able to do. I hope to be able to match the amount of support I've been given by those closest to me, and I'll always aim to share that support with those who need it most.

No matter where I go, I'll always be appreciative of where I began. The clients I met with in my earliest years in Hanford were deeply influential in their openness and sincerity. They invited me into their homes to practice an ability I barely understood, with life-altering results. The fact that Mark and his wife encouraged me to do readings at their store helped lay the groundwork for harnessing and refining my abilities. With every lesson I learn, I think fondly of the wonderful people who started me on my path.

For the amount of support I was given, there's also something to be said about the adversity with which I was faced, and how it helped me get where I am today. I choose to view the difficulties I faced in school as experiences that molded me into the strong, thick-skinned person I am today. People are often afraid of what they don't understand, and there was a lot of misunderstanding from peers about what I did, and who I was.

They helped me better strive to understand myself, solidify my sense of self-esteem regardless of others' opinions, and not take things so personally. That's been a vital lesson, when it comes to navigating all the opinions that get thrown my way today. When we know better, we do better.

In part, this book will reach people thanks to the show, and I want to express my appreciation to the crew and the people behind the scenes who've believed in me and allowed me to share my life on such a large scale. Stephanie and Rasha, thank you for seeing the potential in me and making me part of the 44 Blue family—it's an honor to be able to work with the best people in the business! To Sarah, Jaden, and Anneli, working with you all has inspired a lot of the content in this book, and for that, I am deeply thankful. And of course if it were not for the vision of the team at E! the show wouldn't have the home that it does. Thank you to Jeff Olde, Damla Dogan, Julie St. Aubin, and, now, Adam Stotsky for your unending support. Your questions, discussions, and ideas have all made me take a deeper look at my life and story, in ways I hadn't explored until now.

I want to give my immense thanks to John Edward and James van Praagh, for helping pave the way for the mediums of my generation, and generations to come. They are truly pioneers in the field of mediumship. By the lives they've changed and the minds they've opened, they've revolutionized this subject matter in the mainstream.

Some of the most transformative forces in my life aren't

here physically to read this book, but they are greatly responsible for its creation. My grandmother showed me from an early age what it meant to be loved, and that is a gift I'll carry with me for my entire existence. Tim showed me just how temporary this life could be, and I'll always be reminded how precious it is. Thanks to his existence, even the hardest days are worth being thankful for—and I am. He showed me that you don't have to live ninety years to have a full lifetime. Life is what you make it, in the time that you're allotted. I'll always make the best of it, with you in my heart and mind, until we meet again.

Though I might not know all their names, my guides are massively responsible for getting me here. I'm not always aware of their rhyme or reason, but I don't have to be—their support, and the results yielded, are rewarding enough. I'm just thankful that of all the souls in this universe, they picked me. No matter what challenges may come with living life as a medium, I wouldn't have it any other way. I may never know why I was chosen to have this ability—but I'll never stop using it to share the gift of reconnection. This is about so much more than just me; it's about showing people that love is the common denominator that unites us all, and that we are united eternally. In being able to write this book, I hope that everyone will take something from it and feel more deeply connected to the oneness that encompasses us all. To everyone who has taught and guided me, I am thankful and hope to give back tenfold.

To every person who has watched the show or read this

book, words cannot describe how privileged I feel to be able to share this journey with you, and to be a part of your journey. I hope that you'll voyage on with me, as I continue my quest for answers to life's most important questions—one reading at a time.